Get

Organized!

OTHER BOOKS BY NANCY VAN PELT

The Compleat Courtship
The Compleat Courtship Workbook
The Compleat Marriage
The Compleat Marriage Workbook
The Compleat Parent
The Compleat Parent Workbook
The Compleat Tween
Creative Hospitality
How to Communicate With Your Mate
How to Talk So Your Mate Will Listen and Listen So Your Mate Will Talk
    (Fleming H. Revell)
My Prayer Notebook
Smart Love: A Field Guide for Single Adults (Fleming H. Revell)

Seminar workshops based on *Get Organized!* are available. For further information, contact the author in care of the publisher.

To order, call **1-800-765-6955.**

Visit our Web site at www.rhpa.org for information on other Review and Herald products.

Get
SEVEN
SECRETS
TO SANITY
FOR STRESSED WOMEN

Organized!

NANCY VAN PELT,
C.F.L.E., C.F.C.S.

REVIEW AND HERALD® PUBLISHING ASSOCIATION
HAGERSTOWN, MD 21740

The author assumes full responsibility for the accuracy of all facts
and quotations as cited in this book.

Texts credited to NIV are from the *Holy Bible, New International Version.*
Copyright © 1973, 1978, 1984, International Bible Society. Used by permission of
Zondervan Bible Publishers.
Bible texts credited to NRSV are from the New Revised Standard Version of
the Bible, copyright © 1989 by the Division of Christian Education of the National
Council of the Churches of Christ in the U.S.A. Used by permission.
Bible texts credited to RSV are from the Revised Standard Version of the
Bible, copyright © 1946, 1952, 1971, by the Division of Christian Education of
the National Council of the Churches of Christ in the U.S.A. Used by permission.
Verses marked TLB are taken from *The Living Bible,* copyright © 1971 by
Tyndale House Publishers, Wheaton, Ill. Used by permission.

This book was
Edited by Jeannette R. Johnson
Copyedited by Jocelyn Fay and James Cavil
Designed by Patricia S. Wegh
Cover photo by Joel D. Springer
Illustrations by Mary Bausman
Typeset: 11.5/13.5 Times

PRINTED IN U.S.A.

02 01 00 99   5 4 3 2

R&H Cataloging Service
Van Pelt, Nancy Lue
     Get organized! Seven secrets
to sanity for stressed women.

     1. Home economics.   2. Time management.
I. Title.

                    640

ISBN 0-8280-1327-6

DEDICATION

This book is lovingly dedicated to my daughter,
Carlene Rose Will,
who contributed to it,
who has read the manuscript,
who cares for my grandchildren,
who is surviving and coping,
who is enriching my life as well as the lives of others,
who has experimented with many (if not all) the ideas expressed
and has proved they work—
the type of daughter every mother should have;

and
To all the women
who have attended my seminars
and shared their ideas for sanity with me;

and
To all future keepers of the home,
for whom I hope this book will make it easier.

GET ORGANIZED!

WARNING!

*I*f the clutter in your house is picked up, your bed is made and adorned with 17 perfectly placed Victorian lace pillows, the shower stall sparkles, the miniblinds could pass a white-glove test, the cobwebs are dusted from your front door, and your windows are washed;

if . . . your menus are planned for the next week, and your pantry is well stocked, your closets and shelves orderly, the grocery shopping completed, you can find the name of the orthopedist you used four years ago, your medicine chest is prepared for every emergency and contains no outdated medications, your bureau drawers are freshly lined with scented paper;

if . . . the children's rooms have been redesigned to suit their ages and needs, their toys are neatly categorized and put away systematically, you are never stressed out or irritable, you have energy to spare after accomplishing all the tasks of your day, you are enjoying life, having fun, and are totally organized and fulfilled in every area;

THEN TOSS THIS BOOK!

BUT IF . . . you have trouble getting through the day, you have no master plan for getting daily tasks done, you rarely get the house in working order, you have to plan a month in advance before you can have guests over, your child's room needs a bulldozer before you can enter, the bathroom shelves haven't been straightened since you moved in, your makeup drawer is buried in powder and goo;

if . . . you are behind in everything, and feel totally helpless and stressed to the max, you never have time to do anything *you* want to do, you feel guilty about all the take-out meals your family is consuming, your pantry contains nothing but junk food, and you're too tired to grocery-shop or to cook, you have "to do" lists posted everywhere but you can never get anything done, you are two years behind in reading *Ladies' Home Journal*;

if . . . you haven't washed windows since your college-age child was a toddler, those lumps in the living room that you've been cleaning around all these years turn out to be your husband and kids, and life isn't funny anymore . . .

HANG ON! THIS BOOK IS THE ANSWER TO YOUR DILEMMA!

GET ORGANIZED!

CONTENTS

GET ORGANIZED!

GET ORGANIZED!

BEFORE YOU BEGIN . . .

When reading this book, you may get all kinds of crazy notions about me. You may think I am a Perfectly Organized Person (POP) and either hate me or compare yourself unfavorably to me. The POP exists only in an imaginary world. So please don't get the impression that I am perfect in marriage, parenting, hospitality, organization, or any other topic I have written about.

Not long ago a woman said to me, "Nancy, you're not anything like your books." For one thing, I purposely try to keep a low profile in my own circles; but this woman had made assumptions. She may have assumed that Harry and I have the perfect marriage and never argue. She may have assumed that my shopping is always done, menus arc planned, and dinner is on the table at 5:30. She may have assumed that I am never rushed or behind, that my house is always a perfect 10, and that I never get tired or frustrated.

The truth is, like many of you, I too must cope with the demands of two hectic occupations and still find time for my husband, family, and me. Maybe this woman would be disappointed (or pleased) to know my house does not always score a 10.

I am no more a superwoman than are any of you. But I can tell you that I have a tremendous capacity for getting things done—only because my home and life are organized. When we look at someone else's successes, we tend to assume it was either luck or just came easy for them. We do not see what has been given up to reach those accomplishments.

No one person has all the answers to specific needs, because homes, families, climates, and people are all so different. But by making use of the organizational process I describe in this book, you *will* find answers. I hope you'll continue your search for answers as you refine and define what works for you in your family.

Many women have literally changed their lives by putting into practice the Seven Secrets to Sanity outlined in the pages that follow. Even though the demands of your professional life and the priorities in your home and your personal life are constantly changing, keep focused on the concepts I share in this book, and *your* life will be changed too!

Although I can't be with you in person, I will be there in spirit, cheering you on. I wish you the very best!

THE 7 SECRETS
to Sanity for Stressed Women

SECRET TO SANITY 1:
A WORKABLE DAILY PLAN FOR GETTING CHORES DONE

SECRET TO SANITY 2:
THE FIVE-MINUTE MIRACLE FOR PUTTING YOUR HOME IN ORDER

SECRET TO SANITY 3:
A FAIL-SAFE WAY TO TRACK APPOINTMENTS AND RESPONSIBILITIES

SECRET TO SANITY 4:
MENU PLANNING MADE EASY

SECRET TO SANITY 5:
HOW TO SORT THROUGH CLUTTER

SECRET TO SANITY 6:
HOW TO CLEAN LIKE A PRO

SECRET TO SANITY 7:
TIME-OUT FOR SIMPLE PLEASURES

A woman who lays her daily plans before the Master Planner usually has her priorities straight.

ENTER SUPERWOMAN!

*Y*ou've seen her picture in the magazines. Designer suit. Hair and nails salon perfect. Makeup flawless. Never overweight or flat-chested. Confident smile. Briefcase in one hand and a child in the other, she heads out the door at 7:30 a.m. This superwoman of perfect proportions functions efficiently at the office all day. She is greeted at night by an adoring husband and content, well-adjusted children (who are never sick), who welcome her back to a clean, well-ordered home. Within minutes dinner is on the table. And she's still smiling.

Right. A more realistic picture was shared in a letter to Ann Landers by a woman who calls herself "Tired in Texas." She puts in 40 hours a week at her place of employment and just as many at home. Her supervisory job is extremely stressful, and the demands on her ability during the day are awesome. Everyone wants something out of her. When she arrives at home after a grueling day at the office, she still has to prepare dinner, clean the house, wash clothes, pick up the kids from their daily activities, help them with homework, see that they are bathed, and get them to bed. By that time she is dead tired. Each day gets busier than the day before. She describes herself as "totally shot" and feeling as though she's sinking into quicksand. Her body shrieks *Rest!* but her mind tells her she must get ready for the next day.

"And the real problem is that there isn't enough time to do it all," she concludes.

She paints a pretty accurate picture of all women who work outside the home. Most women work out of necessity. Some work so their family can enjoy a bigger home, nicer furniture, a better car, and more amenities. But the resulting crunch on a woman's time is killing her, physically and emotionally.

Full-time Homemakers

It's not just the working woman who's tired. The full-time homemaker also works hard every day. Not only is she expected to prepare three yummy meals a day, but she must keep up with housework, make phone calls, pay household bills, handle family correspondence, and tackle the mountain of other jobs that bombard her.

If she's a mommy, she must be alert every moment so the child doesn't harm himself or herself or the home furnishings. Once the kids are school-age, she dons her chauffeur's hat. While one child stays for after-school band practice, another has piano lessons, and a third a dental appointment. The master planner of all activities, Mom monitors, schedules, and shuttles everyone to appointments, birthday parties, and family outings.

> *Home is a place where when you need to go there, they have to take you in.*
>
> ROBERT FROST

The larger the family living under one roof, the larger the obligation on Mom's shoulders to keep the house presentable, everyone clean and fed, and activities supervised and flowing smoothly. Stay-at-home moms are also expected to do a lion's share of the volunteer jobs at church and school, as well as become involved in community activities.

Since full-time moms have all day to accomplish this (unlike employed moms), it's assumed their homes, children, and schedules are organized, under control, and in order every hour of the day. In actuality, the full-time mom finishes her exhausting day in much the same manner as does her employed counterpart—just as worn out, and receiving much less credit for her efforts.

The Need? Time!

What women want most is enough time to handle all the required tasks without rushing and feeling exhausted. The need for help in managing their time comes as no surprise to women. When Mom goes off to work, Dad's daily schedule does not change much—her schedule is the one that must be adjusted to accommodate employment, home management, children, errands, and outside activities. Women ask how to combine marriage and a career. Men don't even question it; they assume Mom will handle her job *and* her many home assignments.

Women of all ages enter and leave the job market. They change careers, run their own businesses, have children, marry or remarry, and start, complete, or add to their education. The result is fatigue and a severe time crunch, especially for those who attempt to combine a career with maintaining a marriage and raising responsible children.

Homemaking Styles

Some women cope better with the pressure than others. Why? A *Self* magazine report on American women describes several types of women who share the same priorities in regard to how they want to divide their time for work, home, and personal activities. According to the report, how a woman manages her time is determined by personal values—no one system would be right for every woman. In the study, the women were divided into three categories: the traditional homemaker, the transitional woman, and the achieving woman, labels to help us understand their distinct attitudes.

The Traditional Homemaker. The traditional homemaker plans her life around marriage and children. She has always wanted to be a wife and mother. Caring for her home and family takes priority. A traditional homemaker views work outside the home as a job, not a career. She believes a woman can't be her best when attempting to combine motherhood and homemaking with a career. Her sense of accomplishment comes from raising a family and caring for her home. Traditional values lead her to believe the husband's job is more important than the wife's.

The research concluded that the traditional homemaker is happiest with a 20-50-30 division of her time—20 percent on professional endeavors, 50 percent on home-related tasks, and 30 percent on personal activities. Should that change to a 50-20-30 ratio—50 percent of her time on professional activities, 20 percent at home, and 30 percent on personal activities—she is likely not only to be chronically unhappy and frustrated, but perhaps never to understand why.

The Transitional Woman. Transitional women feel trapped. Their hearts are neither in their work nor in their homes. Most transitional women are married, and many work outside the home. Only 28 percent stay at home full-time. A large percentage of them work because of economic pressure, many at jobs they do not enjoy. This intensifies the strain of having to cope with employment, home responsibilities, and guilt from neglecting the family.

Women in this group feel they have lost control over their lives. Basically, they are traditional in their values and attitudes, but they can't live in accordance with their beliefs. As an escape from their belief system, they tend to act out their frustrations by impulsive spending, excessive television viewing, reading romance novels, and constantly changing their hairstyle and makeup—all vain attempts to reduce the buildup of stress in their lives. Such escapes only create more stress. Because of their impulsive spending, more than 50 percent of transitional women live from paycheck to paycheck.

They lack confidence in their ability to solve conflict and need constant support to help them make life choices. Because these women have never decided whether to focus on homemaking or on a career, they are in a constant dilemma and are perhaps the most confused and unhappy of all three groups.

The Achiever. Achievers know what they want: a career. Their hearts and souls are focused on their work and achievement. They are so work-oriented that they volunteer to chair events, accept new assignments, and take on new challenges. They are overcommitted, overwhelmed, and overworked. They fear losing control—professionally, personally, and at home. So driven is this group that if their act misses a beat, their world comes crashing down. Achievers rate themselves highest on self-confidence, but they face serious time pressures that cause them frustration, anxiety, and conflict. Even so, when surveyed, 85 percent feel their lives are generally happy, probably because of the many rewards their careers provide.

Achievers view their homes differently than do traditional homemakers, whose homes become the center of their existence. Achievers see their homes as an expression of who they are and as a refuge from their busy schedules.

Similarly, an achieving woman would find nothing but frustration if she spent 50 percent of her time on home activities and only 20 to 30 percent on professional tasks. She finds happiness only when she spends the largest amount of her time pursuing professional interests.

Achievers are extremely self-reliant and fiercely independent in a relationship. They can afford to be, because the majority know they could support themselves without assistance. This group is inclined to leave a bad marriage sooner than women in other groups. Family is important to achievers, but their careers and a sense of accomplishment come first.

If you feel uneasy about your life and how it's going, the first thing to do is track how you are living it. Then begin to conclude what *your* value system is—not just a value system your parents may have super-imposed on you. (You may be able to solicit the advice of a close friend or family member. Others can often evaluate things in us that we have difficulty seeing in ourselves.) After you have evaluated your homemaking style, you now must decide: Can I do anything about it? Can I change? Shall I change? Will I change?

Much depends on your circumstances. For instance, if you are married, buying a home, furniture, and cars, and raising two elementary-age children, you may or may not be able to make changes without disrupting the family.

A caution: you must not act selfishly. But understanding what is causing the discomfort in your life may help you achieve some stability by making changes that are possible without major disruption to you or your family's well-being. You may also be able to adjust to your present situation. For instance, instead of moaning about staying home and taking care of children, change your attitude. Tell yourself, "I have accepted this challenge temporarily. I will follow through on my commitment, be a responsible adult, and enjoy fulfilling my responsibilities until such a time as a change can be effected."

> *I just want the merry-go-round to stop, so I can quit being dizzy.*
> KAREN OLSON,
> INSURANCE AGENT

Are you more traditional, transitional, or achieving? The first step to happiness is to discover which category fits your belief system. The next step is determining whether you are living in harmony with your belief system. Then you must do something about it. Choosing to live in harmony with your value system and with what's important to you will produce a higher level of contentment and infinitely lessen stress in your personal life.

The Impact of Organization on Family Stability

As a family life educator, I am convinced that families who follow a simple plan of routine and organization are stronger families. How you use your time, structure your life, and organize your home and time sharply impacts family stability.

Innovative studies prove that organization is essential for family stability. Research now confirms that families are more capable of handling changes and crises when there is a degree of continuity and stability, measured by following established routines, principles of home organization, and quality of family time together.

Four Differing Family Types Identified

The Unpatterned Family. This family has never been organized or developed routines. Furthermore, it doesn't value organization or understand routines. To its members, organization and routine have no meaning or value.

Another term for this type of family is *chaotic*. Chaos dominates when it comes to meal preparation, laundry, order, cleanliness, and structure in everyday life. An example of an unpatterned, or chaotic, home recently came to my attention.

> *A woman who creates and sustains a home and under whose hands children grow up to be strong and pure men and women, is a creator second only to God.*
> HELEN HUNT JACKSON

Donna's mother had married five times. Because of the succession of men who came and went during her developing years, Donna had little recollection of her birth father. Her mother's love life was under so much stress that Mom had little time to nurture Donna or her three sisters. Laundry was done spasmodically. Nutritious meals were unheard of. Meals consisted of peanut-butter-and-jelly sandwiches the girls made for themselves and day-old Ding Dongs their mother brought home from the plant where she worked. Unless an older sister combed Donna's hair, there was no one to care about her appearance. She grew up like a weed, with no structure to her life.

Since she had never been taught principles of order or been required to live by them, she could not find happiness as an adult, and began acting out the same chaotic patterns she'd observed in her mother. Her marriage failed, as did all other endeavors she tried.

The Intended Family. This family sees and understands the value of organization and routine but never gets around to establishing anything. Probably Mom is so busy doing other things she lacks time to organize properly. Furthermore, she lacks discipline and structure in her own life. She has attended seminars and reads books and is certainly no dummy.

Lack of knowledge isn't her problem. It has more to do with organizing her time.

The Intended Family is good at saying such things as "It would be nice to eat a meal together once in a while, but . . ." "We should have worship each morning, but there isn't time." "I know I should get the kids to bed earlier, but . . ." "I really should work out a chore plan so I can get some help from the family, but . . ."

This family talks about making changes, but never gets around to doing anything about it. Good intentions; no follow-through.

The Structured Family. Structured families are organized and have many routines, but there is no meaning to them. Routines are usually rigidly enforced and are performed through habit and tradition, without thought about value or meaning.

Such families are usually formal and cold. No explanations or exceptions are allowed for rigid rules that govern the home. Parents control the home with little consideration for the needs of the individual. Rules are rules and made to be followed explicitly. The parents lack compassion and understanding. There is little warmth or caring here, since rigidity dominates. While such families often look good on the surface, they set individuals up to accept domination and vulnerability.

The Rhythmic Family. The rhythmic family is organized, efficient, orderly, and values the organization and routines established. It's not just having these routines and order that is important. Each family member understands and appreciates the value of the routine and activity.

For example, preparing supper for a child is not just a matter of providing a daily quota of calories and nutrients. Providing a meal can also be a process in which the child is made to feel secure because Mom or Dad provides it at a regular time and in a manner that fosters self-reliance. This becomes part of a tradition or routine that encourages the child to feel important and protected.

An example of a rhythmic family is the Merrill clan. Dubbed "America's Most Organized Family," the Merrills have to be organized, because 21 people depend on Rebecca and Roger Merrill. The clan includes seven children (ages 11 to 27, some married), in-laws, grandchildren, and grandparents. Roger is a consultant at the Covey Leadership Center in Provo, Utah. Stephen R. Covey, the center's founder, is author of *The Seven Habits of Highly Effective People* (Fireside, 1989) and teaches managers to organize their goals by deciding what is most important and never losing sight of it.

Organization is part of the Merrill family's daily agenda. Meal preparation is shared and mapped out in advance, down to the table decorations and the menu. Menus are planned for a week at a time. The grocery shopping is completed ahead of time and nonperishable items held in a large storeroom, where rows of canned food line the shelves.

Another list, "Chores and Bucks," details household tasks that pay. Washing dishes merits a quarter, taking out garbage 50 cents. The Merrills want their children to have a positive experience when getting the job done, not just to get the job done.

Can any family really be this organized? Roger Merrill believes that low-level decisions get low-level results, and that people who make them end up being mediocre. Mediocrity and disorganization are two things this family avoids.

The family has created its own mission statement, something Covey teaches corporations to do. The Merrills recall that the kids' reaction was predictable: "Give me a break!" But they persisted and together came up with a declaration of interdependence about loving and respecting one another.

By their own admission, the key to their efficiency lies in their family meeting. At 6:00 every morning this family gathers in the living room for Bible reading, a short discussion of the verses, and a hymn or song. For a grand finale, they often recite their family mission statement. This is also when tasks are assigned, problems discussed, and discipline problems handled. Most kids wouldn't want to be caught dead reading Scripture and singing with their parents, especially at 6:00 a.m. But it didn't take the Merrill kids long to learn that this type of organization and routine worked in their favor, not against them. The children have grown up with a sense of mission and organization. It's in their blood.

It is Rebecca Merrill who puts most of this into practice. While other women struggle to balance family and career, how does Rebecca keep her many responsibilities from overwhelming her? She works at home as a freelance writer, which allows her more flexibility to shuttle between priorities. But it is only because her household is organized and the children self-reliant that she manages.

Rebecca is busy, yes. But she and her husband still carve out time for each other. Once a month they go out by themselves. Order and organization do not cancel out romance, they say. It might be an evening at the symphony or a dinner in bed by candlelight, but they make time for each other. Once a month they take a married child out to dinner. And once a year the entire family goes on a short holiday together. The Merrills seem to thrive on such family togetherness. Her family happiness "is the result of being organized, effective, and, most of all, principled," Rebecca says.

The Merrill family, like all rhythmic families, is durable and enduring. They can negotiate nearly every life change with relative comfort, because stability has been created through organization and routine.

Structure and organization become even more important during times of crisis. Families tend to lose sight of the value of routine when a child has been diagnosed with a terminal illness and neglect family time and routines. But a family in crisis needs to spend time maintaining stable patterns so that the family unit can maintain its sanity and stability. Without the rhythm, traditions, order, and routine that provide stability, the family is extremely vulnerable.

A Call to Excellence

You're not sure about all this new stuff? You say, "My family has been rocking along fairly well on our own without outside help." You may be doing OK, but mediocre isn't good enough anymore. God calls us to excellence.

The Bible gives us an example of excellence in Proverbs 31 that describes the ideal woman. Some may think this description doesn't fit women today. Few of us deal with merchant ships or have planted a vineyard. And I've never held a distaff. However, God's ideal never changes. His Word is always timely.

Here's my interpretation of Proverbs 31:10-31, put into today's vernacular. The ideal woman:

1. manages the affairs of her household efficiently (verse 27).
2. possesses a noble character (verses 10, 25, 29).
3. is a good wife (verses 10, 11, 12, 28).
4. gets up early and works late (verses 15, 18).
5. has a positive, energetic attitude toward work (verses 13, 17, 19).
6. plans menus and cooks for the family (verses 14, 15).
7. delegates tasks to others (verse 15).
8. conducts astute business deals in real estate, farming, the garment industry, marketing, and retail sales (verses 16, 24).
9. is financially knowledgeable (verse 18).
10. does charity work for the homeless (verse 20).
11. decorates her home in beautiful colors (verse 22).
12. dresses elegantly (verse 22).

13. has a sense of humor, laughs, and enjoys life (verse 25).
14. speaks wisely and kindly (verse 26).
15. is appreciated by her husband and children (verses 11, 28).
16. fears the Lord (verse 30).
17. receives a rich reward (verse 31).
18. loves color and beauty (verse 21).

When you look at all the Proverbs 31 woman was involved in (even though I've taken a few liberties with Scripture), it quickly becomes obvious she was an entrepreneur with a demanding lifestyle. Yet she was also a concerned homemaker and mother to her children, and a devoted wife to her husband. At first glance it looks as though she accomplished it all. And I believe she did—but not all at once.

She knew how to pace herself. What we read in Proverbs 31 is a description of what she accomplished *in her lifetime,* rather than a daily job description or a look at one small segment of her life.

We too can accomplish what the ideal woman did. Max Lucado, one of my favorite authors, talks about the chapters of a woman's life. Then he quips, "And you better know what page you're on."

Four Biblical Principles

We can learn the attributes of excellence the ideal woman possessed by using the following four biblical principles:

1. Do everything in an orderly manner. The apostle Paul recommends, "Let all things be done decently and in order" (1 Cor. 14:40). Powerful words! Words that should guide us daily in everything we do. Wherever we are—at home or at work—do everything in an orderly manner. Have a method and system, a procedure, for accomplishing the tasks of the day. The principle of order will guide us as we attempt to organize our homes and our lives.

2. Do things well. Ecclesiastes 9:10 says, "Whatever your hand finds to do, do it with all your might" (NIV). Whatever task we attempt, wherever we are, and whoever we are doing it for, it should be done well. This means we will take care to complete our daily tasks satisfactorily and properly. If it is worth doing at all, it must be done right. Strive for excellence in everything we attempt.

3. Have a joyful spirit. Paul urges, "Rejoice in the Lord always: and again I say, Rejoice" (Phil. 4:4). While we are getting things orderly, attempting to do things well, and striving for excellence, we must watch our attitude. An interesting verse in Philippians 2 admonishes us to "do all things without murmurings" (verse 14). I really don't know anyone who enjoys scrubbing toilets, but it has to be done. According to Scripture we should do it without murmuring. It may not be our favorite task, but we can still take pride in doing the job well. Having a joyful spirit while we complete our tasks brings a satisfaction and contentment that results in delight and gladness.

4. *Be motivated to achieve your goals.* Some of you may say, "I need more motivation than you'll ever know. I've tried many times to sort my priorities and get my life under control. All I've ever achieved is failure."

This is precisely why we need motivation to try again. Motivation is found in Philippians 3:13: "But one thing I do: Forgetting what is behind and straining toward what is ahead, I press on toward the goal to win the prize for which God has called me heavenward in Christ Jesus" (NIV).

Paul, who spoke these words while he was in prison, had held the coats of those who stoned Stephen, the first Christian martyr. He had good reason for wanting to forget the past. Can any of us equal this for failure and shame? In our role as keepers of the home, we all have past failures. We all live in the tension between what has been and what could be. When our hope is rooted in Christ, we can let go of past guilt and look forward to what He will make of us if we ask Him.

You can't appreciate home till you've left it . . . or Old Glory till you see it hanging on a broomstick on the shanty of a consul in a foreign town.

O. HENRY

Now is the time to forget how often you have tried and failed. Forget the I-can't-handle-it attitudes! Press on toward the goal. Paul could say "I can do everything through Him who gives me strength" (Phil. 4:13, NIV) because he focused on what he was supposed to do, not on past failures. He had his priorities straight and was grateful for everything God had given him. He detached himself from nonessentials so that he could concentrate on the important, eternal issues.

Often the desire for more and better possessions and bigger and greater homes is really a longing to fill an empty place in one's life. True contentment in life is found by examining your perspective of "things," sorting through your priorities, and knowing where your source of strength lies. Christ does not grant us superhuman ability to accomplish anything we can imagine, but we can receive power sufficient to do His will and to face the challenges of our daily tasks. Through each task and time pressure, ask Christ to strengthen you.

No More Excuses

Getting a home "decent and in order" has to do with establishing good habits, rather than constantly caving in to a multitude of excuses why you can't get it together at home. Pam Young and Peggy Jones, two desperately disorganized sisters, have become rich and famous after confessing their faults to the world through their book, *Sidetracked Home Executives*. They listed 155 peanut-butter-smeared excuses for their disorganization. After making their list, they numbered each one. From that day on, whenever they failed, they simply referred to the number instead of wasting time reciting the entire excuse. (Some days were so stressful that the extenuating circumstances resulted in listing numbers 7 through 155!) But no matter how appropriate the excuse, one day they both realized that making excuses for their disorganization did nothing to get them out of the mess they were in. So they stopped making them.

Phyllis Diller, the TV comedian, is another one who invented excuses when she couldn't get it together. She hates housework so much she keeps a desk drawer full of get-well cards, in case someone comes over unexpectedly and she's still in her pajamas at 2:00 in the afternoon. Before answering the door, she quickly spreads her cards across the mantel and in a feeble voice asks whoever is there to excuse the mess, since she is recovering from a deadly bout of the flu.

Stop making excuses! Put that part of your life behind you. All women, whether employed full-time or not, face a severe time crunch.

21 Days to Better Habits

The sidetracked sisters never picked anything up. When they'd get up in the middle of the night to go to the bathroom, they'd nearly kill themselves tripping over evidence of their lazy habits.

According to the *Reader's Digest Great Encyclopedic Dictionary*, habits are "an act or practice so frequently repeated as to become relatively fixed in character and almost automatic in performance." Another meaning is an "addiction," as in being given to, or addicted to, a certain practice. Some people have become so slovenly in their housekeeping that they are addicted to disorganization, clutter, and mess.

One of my favorite self-esteem authors, Dr. Maxwell Maltz, author of *Psycho-Cybernetics*, states that regardless of a person's age or sex, it takes 21 to 45 days to change a habit. Through his work as a plastic surgeon, Maltz discovered that in virtually every case involving amputation it took his patient 21 days to lose the ghost image of the missing limb. He studied the correlation between the human mind and the 21-day period and proved scientifically that an idea or action must be repeated for 21 consecutive days before it becomes permanently fixed in the subconscious.

You may prove Maltz's theory true or false by working to establish new habits. Take the Seven Secrets to Sanity and work to establish them in the next 21 days. Perhaps you, like the sidetracked sisters, will find that after picking things up for 21 days it will hurt your conscience to step over a Lego!

Once you stop making excuses and become aware of your habits, you can focus on the good in yourself. You'll discover that you crave organization, not to impress someone else, but for yourself and for the good of your entire family.

For Those in a Holding Pattern

If you have lost control of your time, or if your life is in a holding pattern, you are malfunctioning. You may be much like the pilot who announced to his passengers, "We're lost, folks; but cheer up— we're making excellent headway." The Bible reminds us to examine ourselves (see 2 Cor. 13:5, RSV) and to know what's going on. "Let everyone be sure that [she] is doing [her] very best" (Gal. 6:4, TLB). Every homemaker needs to seek ways of improving and increasing her homemaking skills that, in turn, will increase the happiness of her family.

One truly affectionate soul in a family will exert a sweetening and harmonizing influence upon all its members.

HENRY VAN DYKE

Many women are functioning in a mediocre manner because they have no plan. A sense of direction can make the difference between responsible living and simply surviving with a group of boarders who happen to be your family. Having a plan puts you in control. Add organizational skills to your plan, and you have the ingredients for vitality and purposeful living. As Christians we know there is purpose and meaning to our lives here on earth. A plan makes a difference, an eternal difference, in what we do and how we act. God has made us stewards of time, talents, and resources

Do you feel that you don't know where to start in bringing order out of the chaos that now rules in your home? Perhaps the thought of drafting charts and lists and following through baffles you. If you feel overwhelmed by household and family responsibilities, you can learn the skills you need to handle them well. It takes determination, but it can be done; not overnight, but step by step. As you master small skills, you develop habits that can last a lifetime.

You must give time to achieve organization and time for yourself. Consider what you are doing as an investment. Just as money makes money, so time makes more time—the one thing most women have so little of! Fatigue and time pressure are two of the greatest problems facing women today, but do not fall for the idea that your busyness is only temporary and that tomorrow, as soon as you get "this thing" out of the way, everything will get better in your life. This is an illusion. Your family is paying an enormous price for this kind of lifestyle and thinking. Tomorrow never comes.

> *Prayer is the mortar*
> *that holds*
> *our house together.*
> TERESA OF AVILA

In this book we will find ways to slow down so we can get more done in less time. We will look for ways to simplify, rather than complicate, our lives. We'll see how to encourage organization, cooperation, and independence in children.

Stay Open to New Ideas

Use whatever you've got at your disposal to make something work. You may think you can't change anything as basic as taking care of the children or cleaning the house, but a new way of doing things could make a big difference in your life. A certain mathematical equation may equal eight; however, there are several ways of arriving at the answer: $4 + 4, 5 + 3, 6 + 2, 7 + 1$, and $8 + 0$. All equal eight. Stay open to new ways of solving old dilemmas.

This book requires more than reading. Nothing will happen until you act on what you read. If you do, it can change your life. Read this book with a pen, marking suggestions you want to try. Modify any principle or suggestion to suit your needs. As you finish each chapter, begin putting that Secret to Sanity to work.

Maybe you're thinking that these ideas might work for other people, but there's no way you can do all this. You're right! If you have never taken the time to plan, organize, and take control of your life, you won't change overnight. But you can change one small area of your life at a time. Success and growth come from a series of small changes that lead toward the goal you have set for yourself. It's never too late to start; it's never too late to change!

For the Organizationally Impaired

Is it possible to become an organized person if you have been disorganized all your life? Yes, if you really want to be. The fact that you have this book in your hand shows a positive attitude toward wanting to improve and change, to move ahead. Choose change and take the first steps necessary to act on a decision.

When you commit yourself fully to a new way of doing things, when you take the first step, you make it possible for God to make you the person He intended. He can bring out strengths you didn't know you had. It is possible for you to surprise yourself continually and live in a constant state of exhilaration and self-discovery. This is what growing is all about.

Time to Commit

It's been said that most of us use only one tenth of the power to act that God has granted us. By committing ourselves to a new course of action, we begin drawing on the other 90 percent. You can achieve anything God puts in your mind as a goal. You can say with Paul, "This one thing I do: forgetting what lies behind and straining forward to what lies ahead, I press on toward the goal for the prize" (Phil. 3:13, 14, NRSV).

Proverbs 16:3 encourages, "Commit your works to the Lord, and your plans will be established" (RSV). If your plans are established, you do not need to become discouraged or frustrated, even when things do not progress as you want them to. You know you are doing what God wants.

If you want to improve, look for even half steps that lead to the change you want to make. Each step may be challenging, but it is within your reach.

Visualize Success

Begin to visualize yourself as a success. If you want to become better organized, picture yourself as an organized person. Let your mind dwell on the advantages of being better organized, rather than on how difficult it will be to accomplish this task. Create a clear mental picture. Visualize yourself successfully moving through the day, efficiently completing each task before you. Picture your morning, afternoon, and evening routines moving along smoothly. Specifically visualize yourself preparing supper from menu plans and ingredients already available, supervising after-dinner chores, enjoying time with your family, and then following bedtime routines. You will find it more likely to happen as you create specific, positive, mental pictures in your mind.

Those who constantly talk about how disorganized they are will continue to be disorganized. By talking about the negative, you give more attention to it than it deserves, increasing its power over you. At the same time you block the organizational qualities you want to develop.

Surround Yourself With Positives

Read inspirational and/or motivational books. Post inspirational affirmations all over the house to give yourself a boost. Spend less time talking on the phone to friends who want to gossip or hash over their troubles. Watch the way you talk to family members and friends. Avoid negative thinking. Fill your mind with positives. Most important, turn off any TV soap operas. Soap operas and romance novels glorify the lives of pathetic people, who are either just getting out of trouble or heading back into it. Focusing attention on so much trouble becomes addictive and robs you of time. In the midst of change you cannot afford to concern yourself with negatives.

Clear your mind of negativity. Refuse to accept one negative thought about yourself or of what you can accomplish. Replace all negative thoughts with positive ones. Carefully read the affirmation you'll find at the end of each Secret to Sanity. These affirmations will help you do this successfully. Photocopy them and put them around the house—on the bathroom mirror, in the window above the kitchen sink, on your desk at work, inside a drawer or cupboard—to remind yourself throughout the day of your determination to think good thoughts, to believe that you can succeed.

Be Patient

Remember, in the beginning everything will take longer to put into effect because you're bulldozing yourself out of years of accumulated stuff and mismanagement. Keep reminding yourself that you didn't get into this mess overnight, and you aren't going to get out overnight.

It takes much less time to establish order in a home and keep it orderly than it does to clean up messes and hunt for lost items caused by disorganization.

Disorder affects every area of your life. It can ruin a good marriage and douse any hope for a troubled marriage. Your finances, social life, and everything else are affected by disorder.

You are getting organized for yourself. When you change something within yourself for the good, only good can come from that change— good for you, your family, and everyone your life touches.

In the beginning, celebrate every improvement made, regardless of how small. Concentrate on the direction you are headed.

Keep Your Plans Mum

You might want to keep your new intentions about getting organized to yourself. The minute you tell your best friend, she's likely to say, "You? Get organized? Now, that's a laugh!" Or "I still remember what happened the last time you tried and failed." If you keep quiet, others can't cause you to doubt your ability to attain your goal. One of the best ways to do this is not to tell anyone—demonstrate day by day what you are up to.

Consult Your Divine Partner Daily

Taking time daily for personal devotions and prayer is absolutely essential in managing a Christian home. Prayer and study of Scripture will provide an advantage as you set priorities. A woman who lays her daily plans before the Master Planner usually has her priorities straight. Regularly submitting your plans to God will help you stick with your goals for as long as it takes to achieve them.

A hundred men make an encampment, but it takes a woman to make a home.
CHINESE PROVERB

Prayer helps control self-defeating habits, attitudes, and impulsive behaviors. Prayer increases faith in your ability to achieve your goals of decency and order. Prayer gives strength to endure frustrations, stress, and occasional failures.

If you've been struggling with getting your devotional life on track, you might want to try an exciting new way to organize your devotional and prayer life. Using a prayer notebook, such as *My Prayer Notebook* (available from the Review and Herald Publishing Association), makes devotional time more meaningful by focusing on a specific type of prayer request each day of the week.

For example, on Monday pray for yourself as a wife, mother, and homemaker; for your career; and for everything that concerns you. On Tuesday pray for your spouse or significant other. You see, you are taking all the things you pray for and dividing them into manageable pieces so that every week everything gets prayed for. This plan for your devotional life follows the same organizational principles taught in homemaking: take a major job and break it into manageable portions to be completed over time.

My Prayer Notebook provides a way to organize prayer requests and answers and will deepen your faith in God as you track His leading in your life. Instructions are provided for making your devotional time more meaningful and enjoyable, as well as providing creative ideas for Bible study.

A Temporary Defeat Does Not Mean Failure

Before Thomas Edison succeeded in inventing the light bulb, he failed thousands of times. Rather than giving up when he failed, he visualized himself being closer to a working solution. Abraham Lincoln was defeated many times when he ran for office. Robert Kennedy failed the third grade and was unable to care for a paper route successfully. Babe Ruth struck out more than any other baseball player, yet he is remembered for his successes, not his strikeouts. Edward Gibson, an astronaut chosen for the Skylab IV mission, failed the first and fourth grades.

Failures, disappointments, and setbacks are a part of life. Successful people understand that. They recognize that even when they take two steps forward and one back, they are still moving toward their goal. We must keep our eyes on our goal and small successes, rather than being swallowed up by our failures.

The beautiful woman is disciplined, chaste, discreet, deferring, gracious, controlled, "together." This kind of woman God considers godly . . .

ANNE ORTLUND

From your mistakes, learn what works and what doesn't. But identify with your successes. Press toward your goal of having a home that is decent and in order. Remain confident of your ability to be more successful and organized in only 21 days. Much of what you will accomplish in the next 21 to 45 days depends on your attitude and whether you believe you can do it.

You can be like the person who is afraid of water and, when seeing a large wave coming their direction, panics and runs, only to be caught, knocked down, and crushed by the cold rushing water. Or you can be like the surfer who anticipates the giant wave, prepares to meet it, rises above it, and rides with its forces to victory!

The Payoff

Experts tell us that as much as 60 percent of our stress stems from disorganization. Once you begin to achieve orderly living, the rewards—both direct and indirect—outnumber the disadvantages. The atmosphere in your home will change; you will notice a new spirit of cooperation.

Security and stability emerge from an orderly approach to organized living, resulting in fewer hours of housework, more time for leisure, and more time for family. This increases the time you have to do some of the things in life you have always wanted to do—pursue hobbies, develop talents, further your education, start a Bible study or women's ministry group, assist at church, volunteer at a worthwhile organization, or take up a sport.

Getting your life and home under control will provide you with a sense of direction, give you control of your time. No longer will you aimlessly drift, helplessly reacting to all of life's events as they buffet you about.

As you plan, organize, and sort through the clutter, you know you are providing the best possible role model for your children. Rather than allowing them to grow up in confusion and disorganization, you are training them for orderly living, providing a greater measure of confidence to succeed in their own marriages and life choices.

But best of all, you'll have a feeling of success and achievement. You'll know that you are a woman of excellence in process. You are becoming a good manager of the time and talents God has given you. You can stand beside the Proverbs 31 woman and look forward to hearing God say, "Well done, good and faithful servant! . . . Come and share your master's happiness!" (Matt. 25:23, NIV).

The next 21 days can be the greatest days of your life. Step out of disorganization into an organized world. Do not allow anyone to cause you to doubt your ability to succeed.

Order in My Life

Every time you successfully complete a Secret to Sanity, reward yourself. After working hard to achieve success in each area of your life, treat yourself to dinner at a favorite restaurant, pamper yourself with a massage, or treat yourself to a bouquet of flowers. Knowing you are going to get a reward when a task is successfully completed helps you face each challenge with equanimity when a planned reward follows.

ORDER

"God is not a God of disorder but of peace" (1 Cor. 14:33, NIV).
"Everything should be done in a fitting and orderly way" (verse 40, NIV).

These verses say to me:

_____

_____

_____

_____

As a result of what these verses tell me, I will

_____

_____

_____

_____

Show off your progress . . .
Bit by Bit!

AFFIRMATION

$\mathcal{T}$oday I choose to put order in my life.
I will ignore negative, self-defeating messages
from the past. I can and will begin doing
things in a fitting and orderly
manner—and it can be fun!

Keep your "Affirmation for the Day" on your desk, a mirror, or the dashboard of your car. It will remind you of your focus for the day and give your spirits a lift.

*H*ave the children pack their backpacks
and have all books, papers, and lunch money set out.

SECRET TO SANITY 1:

A PERSONAL DAILY PLAN FOR GETTING CHORES DONE

s your life in such a whirl of constant activity that you think it would be nice to go back to simpler times? Ah, the good old days . . . before carpools, before you were room mother for 34 fifth-and sixth-graders, before you had to present a marketing plan to six vice presidents of your company. Life 100 years ago must have been a breeze—slow-paced, simple, pleasant, with few demands on a woman's time. Well, let's go back a few years and take a close look at woman's work.

In the early 1900s, according to studies, a woman was putting in about 52 hours a week doing household chores and child care. The figure wasn't much different 50 or 60 years later. By the late 1960s she averaged 56 hours per week. And today's woman continues to work about 49 hours a week on the same tasks.

The odd thing is that when early studies were done, homes had few, if any, of the amenities we now consider necessities. Many homes were not yet equipped with gas or electricity. There were no washers, dryers, or refrigerators. Indoor plumbing was a luxury, and certainly not yet standard in all homes, which meant water was being carried in and out by hand.

The Myth of Laborsaving Devices

By 1950 major technological changes became standard. Indoor plumbing, electricity, and gas had been installed everywhere. During this same time many laborsaving appliances also came into use, including automatic washing machines, dryers, electric irons, vacuum cleaners, refrigerators, freezers, and garbage disposals. In the 1970s and 1980s we added dishwashers, microwave ovens, trash compactors, and central heating and air-conditioning.

Each of these innovations has the potential to save countless hours of labor. Yet none of them has. Studies show that women who have all the laborsaving devices work no fewer hours than those with few. In fact, research suggests the opposite may actually be true. Technical sophistication may *increase* the amount of time spent on household chores. The advance in laborsaving devices has been an abject failure in saving time.

How did this happen? Why have the hours of a woman's work stayed constant, in spite of advancing technology? The answer is simple. In Colonial days laundry was done once a month at most, and in many families maybe four times a year. Everyone wore "dirty" clothes. By the 1920s, when the electric washing machine came into use, people enjoyed a clean set of clothes perhaps once a week. By the 1950s and 1960s it was an accepted practice to wash things after one wearing.

The Cleanliness Bandwagon

Standards have been creeping up ever since for laundry, cooking, care of children, shopping, and cleaning. Estimates in the mid-1970s show the average woman spent 10.3 hours a week getting floors "spic and span," cleaning toilets, dusting, and waxing. Many women today continuously attempt to maintain an eat-off-the-floor state of cleanliness. The axiom "Cleanliness is next to godliness" has been taken very seriously by many.

This cleanliness bandwagon is a modern invention. It wasn't until the late eighteenth century that the people of England began washing themselves regularly. Even then it was only the rich who did so. Body odors and excretions offended no one.

During Colonial days in this country the labor of women was far too valuable to be spent creating a sterile home. The survival of the family was dependent on their making yarn, cloth, candles, and soap. They butchered animals, baked bread, and churned butter. They tended children, gardens, and animals, concocted medications, and cared for the sick. They sewed and mended garments. And they cleaned their homes, generally speaking, only once a year. Rural homes had dirt floors and few pieces of furniture. Open fireplaces spewed out soot. The hauling and heating of water was arduous work, so water was used sparingly for such luxuries as washing dishes. The major effort went into acquiring the necessities—food, shelter, fuel, and water. So much for simple, slow-paced living!

As America grew richer, it got cleaner. Prosperity began to free women from producing necessities, leaving time to devote to housekeeping. Higher standards emerged. Victorian era homes required strenuous cleaning, which was further complicated by the clutter and bric-a-brac fashionable then. By the turn of the century the once-a-year cleaning that homes used to get became an almost-daily event. Every morning women swept, dusted, cleaned, washed, and straightened up. Bigger jobs, such as washing clothes, windows, walls, and baking and canning were done on a weekly, monthly, or seasonal basis.

The new trend also extended to cooking and baking. In early days simple foods (one-pot dishes, soups, and stews) were prepared. But in the particularly labor intensive 1950s and 1960s women learned the art of cooking. Soup and stew gave way to gourmet cooking. Involved meal preparations helped keep women's hours of household chores long.

An interesting phenomenon occurred in the twentieth century. We went from horse and buggy to Concorde; from farm to city to suburbia; from silent movies to videos and VCRs; from manual typewriters to E-mail. Yet through all these technological changes one thing stayed constant—the amount of work done by women in the home. (See the graph below.)

The Constancy of Housewives' Weekly Hours[1]

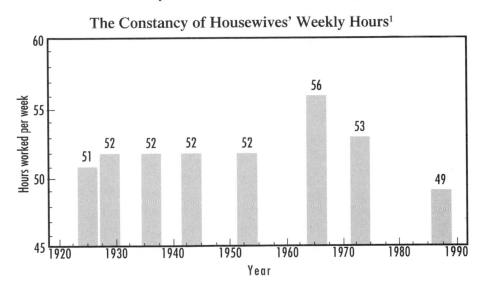

Year

Even as the old tasks disappeared, women took on new ones. Their motto, apparently, was "more and better" as they seemed to observe the Parkinson's law of housework: work expands to fill the time available for its completion. As a woman's time was freed up, her work expanded to absorb her time.

Today's Overworked Women

The situation has started to change, according to Juliet B. Schor, author of *The Overworked American.* Schor estimates that women are finally finding some relief from their arduous domestic schedules because they are marrying later and divorcing earlier. Today's women are also having fewer children. No husband and fewer children reduce the work demands of a home. The number of women who work outside the home also changes the picture. Employed women cut way back on household chores by necessity, doing about two thirds as much housework and child care as their unemployed counterparts.

Since I was 24 . . . there never was any vagueness in my plans or ideas as to what God's work was for me.

FLORENCE NIGHTINGALE

Another factor that figures into the picture is that men are doing more than ever before. Whereas they still aren't helping as much with household tasks (women are still doing about twice as many household chores as men), they are helping more with child care. But things are improving. Every year more men agree that when both women and men work for pay, household tasks should be shared. Even then, 24 percent of employed women are still saddled with *all* the household work, and 42 percent do the bulk of it.

Women who work full-time and have children constitute the group in which the greatest decline in housework hours shows up. Among women with three children there is a drop of two hours per week. Other estimates show the drop may be a little higher. Standards are at long last beginning to slide. Women are contracting with cleaning services to take over big cleaning jobs, and the "clean" bandwagon is in abeyance.

Home Management: A Tremendous Responsibility and Challenge

How does this information translate for today's homemaker? Today's keeper of the home still carries a tremendous load of responsibility, along with many expectations. Managing a family, a home, and children provides a tremendous challenge, as well as opportunity.

Women who are going to be successful managers within their homes need to bring into play many of the management skills used in the marketplace. They may not be dressed in business suits and keep office hours, but they must understand the concepts of team-building, delegation, leadership, age-appropriate job placement, continuing education, and self-discipline, all skills necessary for managers, whether at the office or at home. Every day women follow basic management skills and strategies for achieving results. If you don't have your time-management strategies in place and daily routines operating, there's no way you can maintain order in your home, family, and other responsibilities.

Our family responsibilities may come in different sizes and shapes, requiring that we deal with different issues daily. Yet certain principles, with slightly modified circumstances, can assist us in gaining and maintaining order in our lives.

Where Do We Begin?

The successful management of your home depends to a large degree on your ability to organize what goes on in your home, how quickly tasks are finished, how good you are at deciding what to do (or leave undone), and how well you understand what is important to the well-being of each family member.

Prioritize!

If you sometimes feel you can't keep up with it all, I can assure you that no one can. While you are completing one task, another one is coming undone or coming around to be done again. Admit it: you can't keep up with it all (nor can anyone else).

The commonsense procedure to maintaining a home, then, is to put first things first and get your mornings under control. The woman who never gets anything done, who is always behind, always living in a mess of clutter and unfinished tasks, must break old habits and learn new ones. The good news is that it's possible to learn new work habits and attitudes.

Monitoring Morning Madness

Diana Silcox, author of *Woman Time—Personal Time Management for Women Only*, did a time study for the Gillette Company. She tracked 300 women—working mothers, working singles, and stay-at-home moms—and their use of time from when they got out of bed in the morning until they and/or the last child left the house. The study proved that many women run around the house without a defined strategy.

Typically, women in the study would shower, put on a housecoat, go downstairs to start breakfast, go back upstairs to wake up their husband, go back downstairs to finish preparing breakfast and set the table, go back upstairs to wake up their children, begin a little housework, run downstairs and start a load of wash, vacuum a little, go back upstairs to get dressed and make the beds. The study proved beyond doubt that an enormous amount of time and energy was lost in running back and forth, up and down stairs, beginning several jobs, and finishing nothing. There is a better strategy![2]

One woman, who had no morning plan, said she'd leap out of bed, focused on one thing: getting to work on time. To manage this she did many things in the car—combed her hair, put on makeup, did her nails, and ate breakfast. She never planned in advance what she was going to wear, let alone press her clothes the night before.

> *Organizing is what you do before you do something, so that when you do it, it's not all mixed up.*
>
> CHRISTOPHER ROBIN IN
> WINNIE THE POOH,
> BY A. A. MILNE

Many women in the Gillette study maintained they had a morning routine, but they still found morning hours hectic. One woman complained that her mornings were crazy, rushed, and stressed. She got up at 6:00 and straightened the house. Then she showered and dressed. Next she woke her daughter, got her dressed and fed, and took her to nursery school. She went to her office early so she could sit down for a few minutes to read the paper and catch her breath. Her morning pace is so hectic she overheard her daughter say to a sitter, "We run all morning every morning!"

Many women in the study insisted no time was wasted because there was no time to waste. They simply went through their rushed routines without thinking how to get it all done. Ah! There's the rub. *Without thinking there might be a better way!* When you accept the way you are currently doing things as "normal" or the "right" way, you'll never even think about the possibility of finding a better, faster, more efficient method of completing tasks.

Morning is the most crucial time period of the day for any woman. If you are a working woman who has a husband and children, and you are tackling all this without a well-developed plan, you are likely wasting time and energy. Moreover, you'll leave the house every morning frazzled, tired, and annoyed. You know you don't have your life, your time, or your home under control.

It isn't uncommon to hear a woman say, "Everything is going wrong today. I never should have gotten up." If the day starts off wrong, it is likely to continue wrong all day. If it begins smoothly, it is much more likely to continue that way.

Planning: A Key to Sanity

The key to making a difference in your sanity is to develop a plan for using your time more effectively. If you are practical and realistic, a plan could give you hours in your packed day. You may object, "I'm so busy I don't even have time to sit down and make a plan! Even if I did plan, I don't have what it takes to follow my plan!"

If you don't have enough time to develop a plan, hang on. This plan is different and will work because you set realistic goals that can be carried out. This reduces frustration, so you won't abandon your plan. Rather than taking the fun and spontaneity out of your life, a plan gives you time for more fun and spontaneity.

The only way to be happy with your life is to design a plan for daily living and how you want to live and enjoy your life. *You* determine what type of things will make up and take up your time on that day. A multitude of big and little activities and tasks become the stairway to your Personal Daily Plan. God has a plan for each of our lives and wants to work through each of us to fulfill that plan. He can't do that if His vessel isn't open to receiving or completing His plan.

The only way to get what you want from your days is to plan for it, with flexibility built in. There's no reason to resist planning. You're already an expert at it. All women are. We've been planning all our lives—meals, trips, weekend outings, wardrobes, furniture for each room of the house, activities for the family, functions at church, dinner parties, meeting the needs of husbands and children. With such an extensive background in planning, developing a personal plan for our daily lives should come naturally.

But first we must rid ourselves of negative thinking about a plan. Second, we must slow ourselves down long enough to map out the plan on paper. This can be done in 30 to 60 minutes. Take a lunch hour, get up early one morning, or take a few minutes after the kids are in bed to map out a plan you think might work for your week. The time you spend on this now can save you many hours—yes, even years—of time, stress, frustration, and rushing around. These minutes could change your life forever!

Using a personal daily plan (PDP), you can develop a method of completing daily chores in a satisfactory method that saves time and energy, not to mention your sanity.

The Personal Daily Plan

Business managers of large corporations do it. They get work done through a procedure they call *scheduling,* or a *work plan.* Someone in the corporation maps out a plan and a sequence of steps to be used to accomplish the objective. It works in big business, and it works in the home. Only our objectives are different (housecleaning, keeping up with laundry, meal preparation, grocery shopping). However, both big business and family managers want to accomplish their objectives in the shortest possible time.

Business managers often display a wide variety of charts and graphs to establish a track record of how work is accomplished and the time used to accomplish the end objective. Managers of families can do likewise through the PDP. When sketched out on paper, the PDP serves as a "map" for getting you where you want to go. Most of us are more visual than auditory when it comes to learning a new technique. If we can see it, we can grasp the concept more quickly. This is exactly what your PDP does. Once your PDP is on paper you have a means of analyzing and improving how your time is used.

Five Steps for Creating Your Own PDP

Step 1: Fill in regular appointments and activities. A blank PDP appears at the end of the chapter. Begin filling in regularly scheduled events, appointments, and activities for the upcoming week. Write in mealtimes and regular appointments, such as music lessons, dental/doctor appointments, sports practices, Pathfinder meetings, prayer meeting, work hours, rising and retiring times. These are all activities that are fixed and more or less dictate how you schedule your time.

Step 2: Assign one major task to each weekday. A major task is anything that takes more than 15 minutes to do. Major tasks differ from mini tasks in time only. (Mini tasks described and assigned in step 3 are small tasks requiring only three to five minutes or less.) Major tasks include such things as cleaning the kitchen, vacuuming, dusting, grocery shopping, laundry, and bathrooms. Major tasks do not include daily maintenance (making beds, picking up, preparing meals, cleaning up, etc.).

A major task can be a small block of time five days a week, or a larger block of time three days a week. I recommend a smaller block of time five days a week.

Using the Personal Daily Plan, begin assigning a major task to each day of the week. Feel free to readjust as needed while experimenting with your newly designed plan. Whether you are employed or are a full-time homemaker, it is wiser to portion your work out on a daily basis rather than attempt to complete all major tasks on one day. After completing all your cleaning on one day, you may have a "clean" house, but what about your sanity? How exhausted will you be? How much fun will you be to talk with, to spend time with?

Instead of exhausting yourself in one day, why not consider spreading your workload out over the week? Here's what works for me:

Monday	kitchen
Tuesday	laundry
Wednesday	bathrooms; menu planning
Thursday	vacuuming; grocery shopping
Friday	dusting; meal preparation for the weekend

This is my basic plan. But several major tasks confront me as I go into the kitchen on Monday that could take hours to complete: a thorough cleaning of the refrigerator, washing and waxing the floor, cleaning the oven, cleaning tile grout on countertops, cleaning and polishing wood cabinets. Not included in this list is cleaning out under the sink and organizing drawers, shelves, and cupboards. All major tasks.

A simple secret to sanity includes rotating these major kitchen tasks on successive Mondays, making it possible to have all major tasks completed in approximately six weeks. Think about it! You'll survive if the refrigerator is cleaned only once every six weeks. (If you notice purple goo or furry things bumping around, throw them out!) I usually spend a half hour or so on major kitchen tasks each Monday.

Tuesday is laundry day, requiring a major block of time. Some do laundry every day of the week. I want it done all in one day. I work in much the same way most of you who work outside the home probably do. I toss a load of wash in the washer first thing in the morning while I'm completing other tasks (sheets and towels, so the bed can be remade and towels rehung before my workday begins). As soon as the first load is finished, I toss it in the dryer and begin another washer load. At the end of the day, just before I begin supper, I complete the laundry. By Tuesday evening the laundry is washed, dried, and put away.

Wednesday is bathroom day. Though the guest bath is rarely used, since we no longer have children at home, it still needs weekly maintenance. Fifteen minutes here (tile floor takes longer) and 10 minutes in the master bath (carpeted). Note: Never put carpeting in a bathroom, if you have a choice. It is easier to clean a tile floor, and it's more sanitary. Rotate major tasks in the bathrooms, just as you do in the kitchen. Concentrate one week on scrubbing the shower. Straighten and clean under the sink the next week. The third week, do the floors, etc.

I also plan menus on Wednesday. By Wednesday I usually have a clear picture of the upcoming week, as well as weekend plans. (One of the secrets to sanity is Menu Planning Made Easy. A detailed description of how to get meals on the table pronto is given in chapter 5.) All I do now is sketch meal plans for the coming week into my menu planner and make out my shopping list. Because I have been doing this for years, it is not the formidable task it might be for someone who is just beginning. Usually this is accomplished in 10 to 15 minutes, max. Total time needed for major tasks on Wednesday: 35 to 45 minutes.

On Thursdays I vacuum, rotating thoroughness in each room. This is a heavy day, because I must complete two major tasks: vacuuming (25 minutes) and grocery shopping. One way I save time grocery shopping is by doing a large monthly buying. On the other three weeks I shop for only what is needed to complete my menu plans for the week. A large monthly buying takes about 90 minutes, including driving time and carrying groceries into the house and putting them away. In-store time for a large monthly buying, even when menu planning is completed and I shop by list (I *always* shop by list), usually takes 45 minutes from start to checkout.

Friday is dusting day. I follow the same principles of efficiency as for vacuuming by dusting the entire house in one day, rotating thoroughness of each room from week to week. Every four to six weeks everything that needs dusting will have come full circle in thoroughness.

By Friday afternoon all major tasks are completed. Only on Tuesday (wash day) and Thursday (grocery and vacuuming day) did I run over an hour in time. Excluded from this time frame is maintenance—picking up, making beds, meal preparation and clean up, etc.

Step 3: Assign three to five mini tasks to each major task daily. For example, when I go into the kitchen on Monday to do my major task, it would make sense to concentrate on mini tasks while I'm there. Some that I rotate might include:

- cleaning the inside of the microwave.
- cleaning the outside of the microwave.
- cleaning the outside of the refrigerator.
- cleaning the top of the refrigerator.
- cleaning the appliances (toaster, blender, and mixer).
- rubbing oil into the grouting to make it look new.
- dusting the miniblind.
- cleaning the inside of the kitchen window.
- cleaning and straightening one drawer.
- reorganizing one shelf of the utility closet (located in the kitchen).
- straightening up the cupboard under the sink.

Adding three to five mini tasks to the major task of the day adds 9 to 15 minutes, still a cumulative total of only 40 to 45 minutes for this day. And I will be able to maintain my kitchen at a higher level.

I continue the same practice every day of the week. Wednesday's mini tasks generally focus in the bathroom area—cleaning light fixture prisms, windows, and baseboards; dusting floral arrangements and pictures; or polishing cabinets, reorganizing drawers, or straightening a shelf or cupboard.

By failing to plan, you are planning to fail.

R. Alec Mackenzie,
The Time Trap

Thursday and Friday, while vacuuming and dusting, I add mini tasks from the rest of the house—sweeping cobwebs from the ceiling with a lamb's wool duster, dusting lamp shades and miniblinds, shaking scatter rugs, dusting floral arrangements, brushing velvet chairs, or damp mopping the entry tile. In this way my entire home is maintained over several weeks. I rarely add more than 10 or 15 minutes a day in mini tasks, yet I do five to 10 tasks.

Step 4: Choose a time for major tasks that best suits you. You've picked up the house and gotten the children off to school. So you sit down to have a hot drink and read the newspaper. Then a friend calls and wants you to go for an afternoon of antiquing. When you get home, your day's work is still waiting. You compensate for your mismanagement of time by ordering the kids around and being cross and irritable with your husband.

Where did the problem begin? The first thing in the morning when you lost control of your time. Once you complete your major and mini tasks for the day, the day is yours to use as you desire. A woman who does not work outside the home should always complete her major task the first thing in the morning. If you quilt, go shopping, or anything else before completing your work, the day is already getting away from you.

Don't get me wrong. If you are a full-time home manager, it is perfectly acceptable to sit down for a few minutes and relax—after your major and mini tasks are completed. After all, if you worked outside the home you would have a 15-minute break allotted to you morning and afternoon.

How about a woman who is employed full-time outside the home? She has several options. She can choose to do her major task first thing in the morning, prior to leaving for work, or when she returns from work at the end of the day. Or she might do half the task in the morning and the other half at night. Your Personal Daily Planner is flexible enough to allow choice here. And after your major task is completed, your time is yours to enjoy as you please with a clear conscience, knowing your home is under control. You have completed what is necessary for that day.

> *Prior to planning prevents poor performance.*
> ANONYMOUS

My home is never a perfect 10 on any given day. It takes me a week to get there. I could maintain it at a perfect 10, if that was my goal and I wished to spend the time and energy. But perfection is not my goal. A balanced life that includes family, friendship, hobbies, exercise, and fun is more important to me. Instead of striving for perfection, I've decided to settle for a nice round number, say, 8. When the maintenance of my home slips to what I consider a 7, I get a bit uncomfortable. By the time it slides toward a 6, I'm squirming. At this point I must either get myself back on track or hire a cleaning service to get my home back to my comfort zone.

Step 5: Schedule important things. Urgent happenings often crowd out important things. For example, have you included time for personal devotions and exercise on your PDP? If these things are a priority in your life, they will not be crowded out by other more urgent things clamoring for your attention. If you have it in writing, you are more likely to follow through.

At 6:45 every morning you can see me dressed in a jogging suit, heading out my door for an early-morning fast-paced walk. This is my prime time with God, and only sickness or travel interrupts this appointment. By 7:30 I'm back home, where I take devotional time until 8:00.

If you have three kids to hustle off to school, morning exercise might be out for you, but you could use commuting time for prayer. Over your lunch hour you could devote 10 to 15 minutes for study of Scripture and personal devotions. Or maybe a brisk walk around your office complex, morning and afternoon, will give you some exercise and clear your head. You'll feel better and be healthier.

If it's important to you, schedule it on your PDP. Get it in writing for you and all the world to see. This is the first step in making sure you work an activity into your schedule.

"Routine" Is Not a Dirty Word

Deciding what we want to do each day of the week and scheduling a time to do it establishes routines. Routines help us follow through on what is most important for that day and make it easier to stick to the Personal Daily Plan. Such follow-through also provides a sense of security for children. Not only do they know what to expect and when to expect it, but you're setting an excellent example for their futures.

You probably have established some routines in your family, even though you may not call them that. The secret to success is taking the routines you've already established a step further and make them work harder for you and your family. You'll find it helpful to look at all household tasks, both major and mini, and establish a routine for each one. By pinpointing when each task can, and should, be done and by whom, you can create time-and stress-saving routines.

Establishing a routine that works for you and your family won't happen overnight. Rather, it is a gradual process. There are morning, afternoon, and evening routines. There are school night routines, and routines that govern bedtime, chores, and weekends.

Morning routines. In most homes, morning is the most hectic time of the day. Everyone is getting ready to blast off in different directions. There's little time for positive communication. How family members are launched in the morning makes an enormous difference in everyone's day. It's important that you organize your schedule so you don't have to rush around creating stress everywhere you go. Your children will have enough stress when they get to school. Your husband will have plenty of stress at work. No one needs more stress at home before their day begins—most of all you.

The biggest morning stressors are:
1. Too many things to do in too little time.
2. Arguments with children over what clothing to wear to school.
3. Last-minute signatures needed on school papers.
4. Lunches not ready; can't find lunch money.
5. Hunting for something needed for backpack.

A morning routine can turn morning madness into orderly peace. Here are a few ideas for de-stressing early-morning madness:

1. Pick up the house the night before. Before heading for bed, walk through each room, picking up as necessary. Hopefully you've had the children do this before they retired, and hopefully your husband will also cooperate with this plan.

2. Set the table for breakfast and get the cereal in the bowls the night before. In the morning place the fruit, milk, juice, and toast in easy-to-reach positions. This is a must for women whose children have to be hustled out the door the next morning to school or day care.

3. Prepare lunches the night before. Make lunches immediately after supper. Better yet, have the children handle this task. My four grandsons have developed an assembly line system. Christopher, 12, wipes out the lunch pails and washes out the thermoses. Nick, 7, then dries them and lines them up. Matthew, 14, adds the fresh fruit, while 10-year-old Jamison packs chips and cookies and adds them to each lunch box. My daughter, Carlene, says it eliminates everybody getting in each other's way if each child is responsible for a different task, rather than each child fixing their own lunch. Sandwiches still have to be made in the morning, but having the other tasks done the night before helps the morning rush immensely. The only trick is to get the packed lunches to school with each child!

4. Select clothing the night before. You've had one of those mornings. You overslept. The dog barfed all over the carpet. You burned your fingers on the curling iron. You couldn't decide which dress to wear. A mad search through a jumbled mess of multicolored hose reveals that you got a run in your last pair that matches your outfit. You head back to the closet to make another choice, fully aware that you're going to be late to work. Again.

There is a better way. Make these choices the night before. Not only will you select the wardrobe you will wear, but you also will lay out all accessories needed to complete the outfit—jewelry, scarves, belts, hose, and shoes. A little effort expended the night before helps enormously in the morning, when you might still be a little foggy brained and pressed for time.

5. Give each child an alarm clock. Teach him or her how to set it and be responsible for getting up on time.

6. If more than one child uses the same bathroom, try a rotating schedule with an assigned time for each person. A timer indicates when their time is up.

7. If one child is slower than the others, have this child get up 15 minutes earlier.

8. Put a makeup mirror in a girl's bedroom to free up the bathroom for others.

9. Use a reward system to motivate a slower child toward getting ready faster.

10. Use breakfast as a time to set the tone for an uplifting, encouraging day. Talk about what each family member might face throughout the day and encourage each to do well. Read a short devotional reading, and send everyone off with a prayer especially worded to meet the needs of their individual stresses.

11. Don't turn on the TV in the morning. It's likely to create more stress and distraction from what should be getting done.

12. Create a morning chore chart and post it on the refrigerator at eye level. As soon as the chore is completed, the child can place a star or sticker beside the entry.

13. Offer a reward for being ready for school early. Purchase a special game or toy that can be played with only when the child is ready to leave early.

14. When your child leaves, say "I love you! You are special to me. Have a great day. We'll do something special tonight."

Evening routines. Make sure someone is there to greet your child with a positive message after school. If you aren't there, leave a note expressing that you care. (You can do a week's worth on Sunday night for use during the coming week.) Allow transition time to change clothes, mood, and activity. This goes for you, too!

1. Share responsibility for dinner preparation. One parent can cook while the other plays with the kids. Older children should share with dinner preparation and cleanup.

> *Isn't it interesting that Americans have more timesaving devices and less time than any other group of people in the world.*
>
> ANONYMOUS

2. Schedule routine meals for certain nights of the week to simplify planning and preparation.

3. Make suppertime enjoyable by encouraging the children to tell about their day. Never allow TV during meals, and discourage phone calls. As the ad says: "Don't mess with dinner!"

4. Share cleanup responsibilities with children after the meal.

5. After supper, put all nonperishable items in the next day's lunches. (Some sandwiches can be prepared and stored in the refrigerator.)

6. Schedule a few minutes of fun time with your family several times a week. Play a board game, play catch, ride bikes, build Lego cities. Do something fun!

7. Create a routine for homework in an environment free from too many interruptions. (While the children are doing their homework, you can do yours!)

8. Have the children pick up their belongings around the house before going to bed. Their rooms should be orderly too.

9. Insist that the children pack their backpacks and have all books, papers, and lunch money set out and ready by the door they will exit in the morning.

10. Create a routine for bath and bedtime that suits your needs.

11. If there will be any variation in routine for the following day, go over the next day's schedule with each child.

12. Put the children to bed on time—for your sanity and their best health.

Secrets for a Successful Personal Daily Plan

If a major task is missed, put it off until next week, not the next day. This bit of advice is diametrically opposed to what most efficiency experts advise. Most tell you to make a prioritized list of all tasks needing to be completed. Complete what you can, crossing off what you complete; then leave what isn't done to the next day and continue working down the list. The only problem with this theory is that what laps over into the next day throws you into overload before tomorrow even comes!

My theory works differently. Apportion out your major tasks, one per day, as suggested. If Monday's major task is the kitchen, and you don't get it done because Monday was a holiday and you went away for a three-day weekend, simply put that task off for one week. If you try to do it on Tuesday, along with all of Tuesday's tasks, you'll be overworked. A few days of this, and you'll be ready to lose your sanity.

Wait a minute! What about laundry day? Can laundry be put off one whole week? Not likely, unless you're willing to purchase new underwear and socks. So you'll need to invoke another principle: break major tasks into mini tasks. If you are sick on laundry day and can't get it all done, then do one load a day (and let your family do that!).

How about bathrooms? Can they be put off a week? Of course they can! Apply the same principle. Should you not be able to clean the bathrooms as usual, turn it into a mini task. What needs the most attention? Slosh cleanser in the toilet bowl, do a quick wipe of the counter, and call it quits. Put "clean" off an entire week. It works in an emergency.

Can vacuuming and dusting be put off an entire week? Of course! And please don't tell me you've never done it! These tasks can be turned into mini tasks by skipping them altogether if you've been out of town or have had guests visit. Or turn a major task into a mini task by vacuuming and dusting only the family and living rooms and doing "clean" next week. Your house will not get that much worse as long as you keep things picked up.

This is the secret I use to maintain my sanity. I am frequently gone on a 10-day speaking itinerary. If I leave on Friday (dusting day), I miss dusting, as well as one entire week of my Personal Daily Plan. If I return on Monday, 10 days later, I have also missed cleaning the kitchen. So on Tuesday, when my first normal day at home rolls around, what should I tackle? I'm 10 days behind in everything and feel overwhelmed. Simple! I go right back to my PDP. Tuesday is laundry day, so I strip the beds and complete that task only. In one day I can't make up for being gone 10; I would stress myself and neglect my business. On Wednesday I clean bathrooms and plan menus, and I vacuum on Thursday. By the time the dusting is done on Friday, I'm pretty well back on track. True, the kitchen has only gotten a lick and a promise for two weeks, but I'll catch up on Monday. I'm coping. It took four days to do it, but that's OK too. I'm happy, relaxed, and making sense again.

Be flexible. You've designed your Personal Daily Plan around essential tasks. But allow a time cushion for emergencies that come up, or for those times when you are exhausted and head for bed immediately after supper. Just as planning is the key to time management, so flexibility is

> *Life is what happens while you're busy making plans.*
> ROSEMARY GAILLARD,
> FAMILY SERVICE
> AGENCY WORKER

the key to good planning. You must allow time to deal with the unexpected. Let your PDP go, if you have to. If one of the children breaks a tooth, or if a friend drops by for an unexpected visit, be flexible.

Your Personal Daily Plan must be written out. A Personal Daily Plan is my term for the how and when of everyday tasks. Sketch in your plan for completing one major and three to five mini tasks every day. Once you see your plan on paper, you can improve on it. Having a Personal Daily Plan will help you make the most of your time. And remember, these tasks can be handled as despised drudgery, or they can be elevated to rituals that can be joyful and fun. It's all in the attitude you have toward each task and how you feel about yourself.

All pickup tasks need not be written out, but a PDP should be. Take the blank PDP provided (see page 62) and begin planning, keeping the entire family in mind. Consider not only what tasks you will be responsible for, but what tasks other family members can do to contribute to orderly family living. When designing this master PDP, consider their schedules also. Don't plan on asking your husband to do vacuuming after supper on Monday nights during football season. If a youngster has after-school practice on Wednesday, that is a day to lighten up on jobs to be accomplished.

Another thought: Don't expect your husband to sit down with you and do this planning. If he enjoys cooking and is in the habit of cooking one night a week, ask him what night would work best for him. Perhaps you could use that time after work to run errands. If he detests grocery shopping, why ask him to do it? Instead, ask him if he will take the children to the park while you handle that task.

Any worthy PDP is built around the special needs and preferences of the individual family. Yours will reflect your own standards, as well as the attitudes, interests, financial status, and other factors unique to your family.

What happens when there's a schedule change just when you get your PDP flowing smoothly? Say you're asked to work nights instead of days, or one of the children adds a new activity. Maybe your husband decides to take a night course. With your pencil in hand, quickly begin making changes in your PDP so you can "see" it. The PDP is like a road map to get us where we are going. Attempting to find a new location on verbal directions only can be tricky. But when we have a marked map before us, it's much easier to arrive without incident. Map your changes out on paper.

Rework your PDP until it flows for you. Most of our lives and circumstances are constantly changing, and your PDP must be flexible enough to change with you. Mine changes with the season. In the summer, when the sun comes up early and the daytime temperature soars to 112° F, I get up earlier for my walk and prayer time. In the winter, when it's still dark when I get up, I study first, and then go for my prayer walk.

Don't be discouraged if your first PDP draft seems confining or confusing, especially if you've given little thought in the past to how you are spending your time. With practice you'll soon be able to estimate how long it will take to complete various jobs. You may have difficulty deciding which day works best for which task, and how to group like tasks together so they flow better, but don't expect to make one try at this and have everything operating in perfect sync. It may take several tries before your PDP evolves to the place where it works for you and your family.

One woman designed a plan but complained that mornings continued to be horrible for her. So she revamped it, clearing away every task that didn't *have* to be done in the morning. The children bathed at night and laid their clothes out. In the morning they dressed and fed themselves breakfast. When they finished eating, the children put their dishes in the dishwasher. All she had to do was get herself ready and accomplish a few tasks. Within a week morning became one of this mother's favorite times!

With a list of 10 things to do on Monday, we'd do three, carry over seven; Tuesday add 10, carry over 14, do two; and by Friday we'd have a list of 16,000 things and the baby would eat the list! NO MORE LISTS!

PAM YOUNG AND PEGGY JONES, *THE SIDTRACKED HOME EXECUTIVES*

Personalize your PDP. Look at the sample PDP on page 62 for ideas in designing your own. As you do so, remember that you'll have a far better chance of using and enjoying your PDP if it is realistic and built around your own personality, lifestyle, and energy levels. Figure out your peak performance time (are you a morning or evening person?), and utilize it to your advantage in completing major tasks.

The commonsense procedure for maintaining a home, then, is to put first things first. There will be times when a clean house is far down on your list of priorities, far behind other matters of family living. Emergency and impulse occasions will arise when you chuck housework in favor of spending an evening out with friends. Illnesses will occur during which you pass viruses around to each other and everyone in the family is sick for weeks at a time. At such times you settle on household tasks that are essential and concentrate your remaining energy on survival.

Quick Tips for Making a Personal Daily Plan Work

Include personal time. Routines must include personal time and go beyond reducing chaos and getting chores done. When you work full-time outside the home, the law decrees that you get a break every two hours. Studies on work habits show that productivity goes up and accidents go down when workers take a periodic break from their labor.

The same is true in the home. Studies on homemakers indicate it is important to rest from housework before one becomes too tired. Write personal time into your PDP. Take a short break when you begin to tire. If you push through the exhaustion to completion, it takes longer to recover energy. Lie down with your feet up for 10 minutes. Phone a friend. Write a note or read a book. Quilt for a few minutes. Don't feel guilty for treating yourself in this way—it will benefit you in the long run and save your sanity. Anticipating something fun will also help you whisk through your chores.

Lord, help me find the time to meditate on the most important relationship of all—my relationship with You. Amen.

ANONYMOUS

Schedule time for the family. Be sure you schedule one night a week in your PDP for family time with your husband and children. Spend one uninterrupted hour after supper doing something with them. Call a family meeting and ask your family to make a list of fun activities they would like to do, then work from this list. It's guaranteed your children will love to add their ideas. You don't want to be so busy endlessly "doing" that there is no time for "enjoying."

A Personal Daily Plan for Children

Children need a personal daily plan too! Has one of your darlings ever said, "But I didn't know I was supposed to do that"? If so, it's time to send a clear message about what is expected. If your expectations aren't clear and nothing is expected on a regular basis, the child is not developing responsibility. Some moms ask for help only when it's needed. Other moms feel guilty for working outside the home and think it unfair to ask children to handle tasks they, as full-time moms, used to do. Still others are afraid children might resent the fact Mom works outside the home if they have to do part of her work.

This is all faulty reasoning. Whether you work outside the home or not, there's no reason you should make your children's bed, pick up their clothes, or do their chores. From the time they're small, children should become responsible for more and more of their own care. The first tasks to appear on a child's Personal Daily Planner are those tasks that must be done daily. If daily tasks appear on their PDP, instructions for such tasks will not have to be repeated daily.

Routine tasks might include making beds, hanging up clothes, putting laundry where it belongs, and putting toys in their proper place. By doing these tasks routinely, the child is learning to take care of their own daily living. Habits taught early become an accepted standard of living. Remember, if you are not teaching specific good habits, your child will learn negative habits. If you are not teaching your child to pick up their clothes, they are learning to leave them where dropped. If your child is not taught to help with household chores, they are learning that they are not required to contribute to general family living.

Besides routine tasks, more specific jobs need to be assigned to keep the household running. Setting the table, meal preparation, loading the dishwasher, and taking out trash should be negotiated before decisions are made. Detested jobs can be rotated. When discussion is over, jobs should be clearly assigned, clearly understood, and written out on the child's PDP or job chart. Each family member will have certain jobs that need to be done regularly. There should be a clear understanding among all family members that everyone in the family depends upon him or her to do this.

If a child's task is to empty trash, they must understand when and how the task is to be completed, and that it is to be done before they can play. They must also understand what days trash is collected, and that garbage cans are to be placed at the curb. Clear instructions must be given about what to do when trash falls from a wastebasket, about putting empty containers back in their places, and where and how to handle kitchen trash containers. When the dimensions of the job are clearly understood by the child, they know what the job is, when it is to be done, and what is involved in doing an acceptable job.

If a child is to put their own laundry in the washer, teach them how to operate the appliance and give directions regarding the use of detergent. If they are expected to remove clothes from the washer and put them in the dryer, they must be told why it is important to do so immediately, and why they must later be removed from the dryer immediately.

It is up to you, as the family manager, to see that routine jobs are completed daily. Tasks cannot be skipped just because the child got up late or it was inconvenient for them or for you. Occasionally Personal Daily Plans need to be changed, but don't change the plan until it has become a habit. (Remember, this takes 21 to 45 days of continuous repetition). This learning process is not easy for the parent to supervise, and it becomes increasingly difficult for the parent of several children, or for one who must hustle off to work. But the more hectic your schedule, the more necessary it is for you to keep PDPs in place for the running of your lives and home. Children cannot thrive in the midst of chaos.

Even older children (10 to 12 years old) who have never been taught organizational habits will willingly follow a PDP when introduced to it through a family meeting. Encourage them to develop their own plan. See examples of a child's daily planner at the end of this chapter (younger children on page 63; older children on page 64). Offer help or suggestions as needed. When beginning, encourage as much input from them as possible. It will be easier to teach the concepts of a PDP to your child if you follow one yourself.

PDP Benefits and Rewards

A PDP is more than just a list of jobs to do whenever you get around to them or feel like doing them. It is possible to get more done in less time once you get your Personal Daily Plan functioning, because it organizes tasks to be done and the time in which to do them—a must for any woman who wants to control her time and cut down on wasted effort and indecisiveness. Rather than taking the fun and spontaneity from life, a PDP collects time in usable amounts. It puts you in charge of your day, rather than allowing you to remain a victim of it.

A PDP cannot work without determination, especially at first, when you have been used to doing what you want to do when you feel like doing it. But the rewards are tremendous! The confidence and peace of mind that come from an orderly plan for dealing with the demands of managing a home are worth it.

Staying with your PDP may stretch you to capacity at first, but after a couple weeks you should discover that it gets easier. If your PDP doesn't work after four weeks, take it back to the drawing board and redesign your plan. The principle of dividing major and mini tasks up among the days of the week always works. What may have to be redesigned is how the tasks are divided and when they need to be completed. Once you get your design on paper and get it rolling, it will become easier.

---

[1] Estimates from 1926-1927 through 1965-1966 are from Joann Vanek, "Time Spent in Housework," *Scientific American* 231 (5 November 1974): 116-120. Estimates for 1973 are author's calculations. All data are for full-time workers.

[2] Juliet B. Schor, *The Overworked American: The Unexpected Decline of Leisure* (New York: Basic Books, 1991), pp. 83-105.

MY PERSONAL DAILY PLAN

TASKS	SUNDAY	MONDAY	TUESDAY	WEDNESDAY	THURSDAY	FRIDAY	SATURDAY
Major Task (one major cleaning task per day)							
Mini Task (three to five mini tasks per day)							
Mini Task							
Mini Task							
Mini Task							
Mini Task							

A CHILD'S OWN PERSONAL DAILY PLANNER (AGES 6-9)

BEFORE SCHOOL:

6:10-6:30	Personal Devotions.
6:30-6:50	Shower.
6:50-7:00	Make bed.
	Pick up/put away *all* personal items.
	Pick up bathroom.
	Get dressed.
	Comb hair.
7:00-7:20	Eat breakfast.
	Clear dishes to dishwasher.
7:20-7:35	Pack lunch.
	Brush teeth.
	Tidy sink, toothbrush, comb.

AFTER SCHOOL:

3:00-3:30	Change clothes.
	Hang up clothes/put in laundry.
	Put away shoes.
	Pick up bathroom.
	Make lunches.
	Get table set for supper.

DAILY JOBS:

3:30-4:00	Get all homework done.
4:00-6:30	FREE TIME!
6:30-7:00	Supper.
	Clean up after supper.
7:00-7:30	Listen to *Odyssey* on the radio.
7:30-7:40	Set table for breakfast.
	Fold clothes and put away or in laundry.
	Pick up *all* personal items in room and put away.
	Check clothes for tomorrow.
	Brush teeth.
7:40-8:00	Worship. Put Bibles away.
8:00-8:30	Personal reading.
8:30	LIGHTS OUT!

A CHILD'S OWN PERSONAL DAILY PLANNER (AGES 10-12)

	Sunday	Monday	Tuesday	Wednesday	Thursday	Friday
	Garbage to the street	Laundry		Garbage to the street		
		Empty dish-washer			Empty dish-washer	
		Clean bathroom / Wipe down toilet / Wipe floor by toilet / Vacuum floor / Wipe counter / Clean sink				Clean bathroom / Wipe down toilet / Wipe floor by toilet / Vacuum floor / Wipe counter / Clean sink
	Clean fishbowl				Clean fish bowl	
	Feed bird	Feed bird	Feed bird	Feed bird	Feed bird	Feed bird
	Clean up Legos			Clean up Legos		Clean up Legos
	Vacuum room					Vacuum room
	Care for cat	Care for cat	Care for cat	Care for cat	Care for cat	Care for cat
		Vacuum family room/kitchen				
	Bake bread			Bake bread		
	Wash car					

The Personal Daily Plan

Assignments:

1. Sketch in your plan for completing household tasks on your Personal Daily Planner. Include one major task and several mini tasks per day. Remember to schedule personal time every day. Then enjoy the benefits of having your work load portioned out, "decently and in order."

2. For personal devotions, read Jeremiah 29:11-13: " 'For I know the plans I have for you,' declares the Lord, 'plans to prosper you and not to harm you, plans to give you hope and a future. Then you will call upon me and come and pray to me, and I will listen to you. You will seek me and find me when you seek me with all your heart' " (NIV).

This verse says to me: _____

_____

_____

As a result of what this verse tells me, I will _____

_____

_____

Don't wait for motivation to come.
Motivation comes once you begin!

AFFIRMATION
for Secret to Sanity 1

*T*oday I choose to put order in my life. I will take charge of my time, and by so doing I can also change my circumstances. I choose, by the grace of God, to have a plan for this day. I choose to become more efficient in my use of time, thereby fulfilling my desire to work more efficiently in my home. It can be done, and it can be fun!

Lift your spirits—go the extra mile

1. Often we allow urgent happenings to crowd out important things. If you haven't already done so, schedule time for exercise, family, and yourself on your Personal Daily Plan.
2. Before you go to bed tonight, pick up each room. See what a difference this makes tomorrow morning!
3. If you have children who must be hustled out the door in the morning, at least two times this week set the table for breakfast, prepare lunches, and select clothing—all the night before. Small tasks completed the night before can make a big difference in the morning.
4. Plan a fun activity for yourself this week.

The Five-Minute Miracle is based on first appearances. There is a sense of order and welcome, even though the room may not have been "cleaned" for a week or more.

3

THE FIVE-MINUTE MIRACLE FOR PUTTING YOUR HOME IN ORDER

he house is a disaster area, with a barely discernible pathway threading away toward the bedroom. The bedroom door barely cracks open against a backwash of clothes tossed wherever, scattered toys, laundry, shoes, dirty dishes, and a host of other unmentionables. Your nerves are frazzled and your temper is short. You'll have to take a day off work and rent a bulldozer to find floor level.

Hold it! There is an easier way—The Five-Minute Miracle.

Here's how it works: Before leaving for work or school or beginning your duties of the day, devote five minutes to straightening each room before you leave it. Where to begin? I suggest the bathroom.

The minute your morning routine is completed, do a quick cleanup in the bathroom. Hang up the towels. Put countertop clutter back in the drawer. Use a wipe to clean toothpaste or hair residue out of the sink quickly. Pick up clutter that's been dropped on the floor. This is not the time to scrub toilets, scour showers, mop floors, or dust prisms dangling from light fixtures. The object is to restore order before leaving the room, and picking up restores order quickly, in most cases in five minutes or less.

Next, pick up the bedroom. Put clothes and shoes away in the closet. (Of course, had this been done the night before, you wouldn't have to do it now. But then, some of us learn the hard way!) Fold nightclothes and put them under the pillow or in a drawer. Make the bed and straighten the pillows. Pick up newspapers and any dishes carried into the bedroom the night before. Discard paper clutter that has accumulated from the previous day on a nightstand or dresser top. Now look at your room. It may not be *clean,* but it looks orderly, inviting, and pleasant. Visible clutter has been put away.

Teach this same concept to the children. Once dressed, they spend five minutes picking up. (Don't call it cleaning. Children immediately resist "cleaning their rooms.") This includes making their beds, putting shoes, clothes, and toys away in their proper places—from the biggest, most visible items to the smallest. Only five minutes are allowed to accomplish this. Five minutes (or less) must also be spent in the bathroom hanging up towels, putting things away, and cleaning up messes.

Form good habits. They are just as hard to break as bad ones!
ANONYMOUS

You can eventually turn daily pickups in general living areas over to them as well, once the principle is learned. And children will learn this more quickly if there are consequences attached. For instance, no breakfast until these two five-minute jobs are accomplished. Growling tummies are more effective in getting all the tasks done in short order than all the nagging harangues given by most mothers as they hustle children off to school.

If breakfast cereal was poured into the bowls the night before, children can easily get milk from the refrigerator and begin breakfast at the appropriate time. You can breeze in with a smile on your face and a pleasant greeting, for your day has been given a head start. Sit down with the children and share a short devotional reading and prayer—something pertinent to their life—and set a pleasant mood for their day.

When breakfast is over, have each child rinse his or her own dish and put it in the sink or dishwasher. (Husbands can also learn this quick trick.) Require that everyone do one more task to keep the kitchen clean—one person puts the cereal away, one the milk, another the juice, while someone else gives the floor a quick sweep to catch spilled Cheerios.

You can leave for work confidently, knowing your home is in order, and feel good about yourself and your home all day. If you are a homemaker, once the children are off to school you are free to begin your one major cleaning task for the day. Since clutter has already been put away, you can happily face this task. It is infinitely more difficult to face a major cleaning project when you are surrounded by unmade beds, dropped clothes, wet towels dangling drunkenly from the ends of beds, and scattered toys and clutter everywhere.

Celebrated interior designer Alexandra Stoddard asks an interesting question about the home: "Does your home smile at you?" That's exactly what a picked-up, decluttered home can do for anyone entering it. After a hard day it is discouraging to enter a home that is in total disarray. It is difficult to begin preparing the evening meal until the kitchen is picked up first. When that task has to be completed before meal preparation begins, you are already one task behind, and you've barely entered the door!

That 15 to 20 minutes you spend in the morning picking up the bathroom, bedroom, and kitchen and helping the children makes the difference in how you feel about yourself throughout the day. But the most remarkable change you feel is when your home welcomes you with a "smile."

The Five-Minute Miracle is based on first appearances. When guests visit your home unexpectedly, they rarely check the carpet to see when you last vacuumed. Neither is a white-glove test given to wooden surfaces for dust, nor windows eyeballed for streaks and spots. What a guest first sees when entering a room is *order*. If things are in their place, picked up, put away, wiped off, and straightened up, the room gives off the impression of being clean. There is a sense of order and welcome, even though the room may not have been "cleaned" for a week or more. An orderly house gives you a feeling of confidence and accomplishment, regardless of when you last cleaned. Order is rewarding and generates success.

Avoid the Tendency to Deep-clean

The Five-Minute Miracle isn't the time to scrub and polish the kitchen floor, clean out the refrigerator, shampoo carpets, or clean the hall closet. These things may need doing, but must be tackled during cleaning time. If you stop to clean the hall closet now, you will be tackling a major cleaning task that will create a huge mess, and the rest of your home will be messy too. However, should the hall closet be your major task for the day, pick up first, then proceed with the closet.

Work From the Outside In

Enthusiasm may strike to clean a cupboard, closet, or drawer during the Five-Minute Miracle. Resist it! Always work from the outside in. Clear clutter before digging into a drawer. Starting with the closet makes a double mess. You'll likely get discouraged and quit before either job is finished.

Designate Several Pickup Periods Throughout the Day

Pick up before the mess becomes monstrous. If the children have been playing in the family room, have them pick up their toys before going out to play. Have them put their outside playthings away before coming back in. Allow time for other pickup periods before eating, naps, and going to bed. This principle applies to every member of the family, not just small children!

Pick Up in the Morning

The ideal time to accomplish this daily run-through is in the morning, before you leave a room. There are many variations that might be possible, but the important thing is that every day every room gets some attention. Do make your plan flexible, however. A parent of small children who has many interruptions can accomplish this in five-minute bites.

I can hear some of you saying, "You don't understand. My home is a major disaster area, a candidate for one of those bulldozer jobs you talk about. Picking up just won't work." Picking up can help, even in this situation. It keeps things from getting worse until you arrange for the bulldozer!

Picking up is a principle that can be activated quickly and can make the greatest visible difference in your home in the shortest amount of time. Remember: keeping up is easier than catching up. Avoid feeling so defeated by a tornado-struck room that you do nothing. The room may look like it will take hours to restore order, but a few minutes of picking up will keep it from getting worse. You can clean later, once you get things put away. Monday will probably be the hardest day, especially after the irregularities of a weekend schedule. Get everyone back on track Monday morning, and see how each day becomes easier as you move through the week.

Keeping up keeps you going, gives you hope. Develop the habit of putting things away before going on to something else, while they are still in your hand. A woman who attended one of my organization seminars told me that to get motivated to pick up first thing every morning she played a mind game, imagining that her mother-in-law would be dropping by soon. If a mind game like this works for you, use it. However, remember that you are picking up your home to please yourself, not someone else. *You* are the one who is benefited and blessed by self-esteem and sanity.

By practicing the Five-Minute Miracle every day, you can put house-cleaning on hold for a long time simply by keeping up with laundry, meals, and dishes. Essentially, this is how the woman who works full-time outside of the home survives. Of course, eventually you will have to go beyond picking up to cleaning. And the secret for that is found in understanding what has to be done and maintaining a manageable Personal Daily Plan chore schedule. In the meantime, the Five-Minute Miracle gives immediate results.

This simple Secret to Sanity can make the biggest, fastest, and most visible improvement in your home!

Benefits of the Five-Minute Miracle

1. It maintains your home and keeps things from getting worse.
2. It boosts your self-worth.
3. You enjoy your home more.
4. Areas you have already cleaned will stay clean and be enjoyable longer.
5. You can move more easily into deep cleaning and other tasks.
6. It is an easy principle to teach to your spouse and children.

The Five-Minute Miracle

Assignments:

1. Practice the Five-Minute Miracle pickup plan daily, beginning today.

2. For personal devotions read Proverbs 14:1: "The wise woman builds her house, but with her own hands the foolish one tears hers down" (NIV).

This verse says to me: _____

_____

_____

As a result of what this verse tells me, I will _____

_____

_____

Home is not given, but made.
Father, light up the small duties of this day.
May they shine with the beauty of Your presence.
May I find glory in the small common tasks before me. Amen.

AFFIRMATION
for Secret to Sanity 2

Today I choose to put order in my life.
I request and accept energy from God to
accomplish the many tasks before me.
This is my day, my time, and my home.
I will joyfully restore order in each room
and have a positive attitude while I do it.
It can be done, and it can be fun!

Lift your spirits—go the extra mile

1. If you are so stressed that even your prayer life has dwindled to a disorganized hit-or-miss schedule, try *My Prayer Notebook.** This beautifully designed notebook divides prayer topics into manageable portions by assigning topics to days of the week. For example, pray for yourself on Mondays; your husband or significant other on Tuesdays; and on Wednesdays, your children and extended family.

2. One night this week go to bed one hour earlier than usual. The next day get up one hour earlier and spend a few minutes alone with God. Getting up early will give you a jump on the day. One peaceful hour spent alone can be worth more than three hours fractured by interruptions later on. You will feel more rested and relaxed from going to bed early, spending time with God, and thinking through and praying about your day.

3. Work smarter, not harder. Tackle the most difficult tasks first or when you have the most energy. When you are tired, you can still tackle mini tasks, put things away, and putter. Quit while you are ahead and come back refreshed.

My Prayer Notebook, published by the Review and Herald® Publishing Association, Hagerstown, Maryland, is available at Adventist Book Centers. Order by phone at 1-800-765-6955.

Determining an area in your home from which you can manage your family more efficiently will help you as well as your family.

4

A FAIL-SAFE WAY TO TRACK APPOINTMENTS AND RESPONSIBILITIES

ou missed the doctor's appointment that you waited two months to get. And if you'd been on time for Matt's dental appointment last week, you wouldn't have had to spend a whole hour reading outdated, torn-up magazines in the waiting room before the dentist could work you in.

Oh, and you can't forget to pick up the kids at 4:30, and take Chris to his music lesson at 5:00. Be sure to pick him up at 6:00, so you can drop him off at Pathfinders at 7:00. The other kids need to be at the church at 6:30 to practice for a skit.

Excuse me. Your doorbell is ringing.

"Why, Sean and Michelle! How nice to see you. But why are you here? Dinner? *Tonight?*"

You've got so many calendars and lists and scraps of paper all over that you need a secretary and an office to keep it all straight. Good news! You *can* have your own efficient office that will run itself—and without an expensive secretary. Other than a little straightening up once in a while, it doesn't need cleaning, and it's small, colorful, and attractive. Best of all, it tracks appointments, phone numbers, and volumes of other information you need to run your life and home. It completely removes the responsibility for remembering from your shoulders.

What is this wonderful office? A personal planner book! You say you tried that before and hated it? It was too big? And ugly besides? Well, how about a planner that's so small it will fit easily into your purse, yet is big enough to keep track of everything that's going on in your life? It's so easy to set up that you can have a lifetime system in place in one evening. And it's affordable and attractive too.

Years ago I attended an organization seminar at which a personal planner was marketed. I liked the idea of getting organized and knew I needed a system, but if I got something, it would have to be lightweight and portable—and pretty. It had to go everywhere I went, and it had to be small enough to fit in my purse.

> *There cannot be a crisis next week. My schdule is already full.*
> HENRY KISSINGER

There are a number of planner systems available, such as Day Runner, Franklin Day Planner, Day-Timer, and Day Minder. My personal choice is Day Runner's Slimline System, a six-ring binder 3¾" x 6¾". It's available in either a less expensive vinyl, or a more expensive tapestry and leather. I've used the more expensive binder for five years with excellent results. The tapestry fills my need for beauty and elegance, and the leather is rich-looking and long-lasting.

Tracking Weekly Activities

The first thing a personal planner must have is a calendar. Since I don't have multiple appointments every hour of the day, I prefer the week-at-a-glance calendar. I keep the pages for only three or four months in my planner, rather than the entire year. This keeps my planner slim.

On Sunday night or Monday morning I map out all appointments for the upcoming week. A ruler, which doubles as a bookmark and is slightly taller than the calendar page, easily pops in and out of my planner and is moved from week to week. (Hint: Whenever you write down an appointment, lunch date, or meeting on your calendar, include a phone number for future reference should you need to cancel or reschedule.)

My daughter, Carlene, keeps a lined page between each calendar week, on which she jots down things that need to be done that week but not completed on any certain day. With four boys to keep track of, her schedule gets very hectic, and this list helps her remember without locking her in.

The rest of my system is set up around seven tabs. I recommend purchasing blank ones and designing your own. Manufacturers usually arbitrarily title tabs *"Finances," "Projects," "Objectives," "Notes,"* etc. This does nothing to organize my life or the lives of most women I know. Purchase tabs with labels on which you can print what you want. For example:

> Personal Information
> Committees
> Business
> Items Lent and Things to Remember
> Medical
> Household Information
> Sermon Notes and Prayer Requests

Personal Information

For quick reference I keep a couple pages of frequently called numbers (no addresses or other information) of friends and those whom I call often. These two pages are the most frequently used portion of my personal planner.

Following these pages are source pages—family. On two sides of one page appears the address, phone, fax, cell phone, and E-mail information for every family member. You might want to write this information in pencil, rather than pen, since phone numbers change and people move.

Next I record all miscellaneous personal phone numbers and information—my travel agent, a housecleaning service I use occasionally, my Mary Kay dealer, the Fresno Bible House, the local Christian radio station, a Christian financial counselor, an auto repair shop where Harry gets work done on the car, our bank, a place I take clothes to sell when I get tired of them, and my hairdresser. It's been three years since the trees in our front yard were trimmed. I just saved myself tons of time by checking my planner and calling the number of the service I used three years ago.

Also in this section, on two sides of one page, I list by month all birthdays and anniversaries that I like to remember with a card or gift. At the first of each month I quickly check the list for upcoming events and make plans to care for them appropriately.

Committees

Record every committee or group of which you are a part. Here is where you would find my prayer group and women's ministry committee, along with every address and phone number necessary to reach each member, should there be an emergency or change of plans. Some women photocopy their entire church list at a reduced size, then cut pages to fit their planner, six-hole-punch them, and have ready access to the entire church.

Business

My business is publishing and seminars. So on the first page of this section, on a lined sheet, I list all frequently called publishers and business associates, with phone and fax numbers. I list information on each publisher on the source pages that follow, including the names of editors and publicists. On another page are all other suppliers from whom I order, literary agents, and other authors whom I might need to contact.

Items Lent and Things to Remember

Items Lent. Now, don't laugh! The purpose of a personal planner is to de-stress your life and free your mind. How many times have you lent an item to someone but can't get it back because you can't remember to whom you lent it? The plan is simple: every time you lend something out, jot down the date, the item lent, and to whom you lent it. When it's returned, cross it off. Simple plan. Marvelous results.

Things to Remember. A family manager must track a multitude of trivial information in order to keep her world humming. It's easy for her mind to become cluttered and slip into overload. So free your mind by jotting down trivial information, and let your brain move on to solving other important tasks. The type of information found under this heading might include: which exit to take for the mall; the name of a new night cream I tried and liked and will purchase again; a good cookie I had on the plane and want to purchase; a cleaner's in town that specializes in handling special cleaning problems; the street UPS is on (I added this after getting lost twice and wasting untold time by having to stop and ask for directions).

Every trivial bit of information that doesn't fit into other categories gets jotted down here.

To this section I've also added a page entitled Books to Get. In my travels, people often recommend books to me. Rather than jotting the title on a scrap of paper and cluttering my briefcase or purse, I jot it on a page in my planner. As I read such books, I cross off the title.

This is the place I list local restaurants that people recommend to me. When Harry wants to take me out for a special occasion, or when friends come to town, I have some new ideas, rather than always going back to the same place.

I use a similar method for videos. There's one thing on which Harry and I rarely agree: what video to rent for an evening's entertainment. So we've put together a list over the years, and this is what we rely on, crossing them off after we've watched them.

Medical

Here you list the physicians and dentists you and your family see, along with addresses and phone numbers. I take this a step further by writing a brief description on source pages regarding the nature of each visit and the results. For example, an entry might read: "On July 11 I saw Dr. Suchy. Diagnosis: bronchial asthma or allergic bronchitis. Put on inhaler. Claritin 10 mg. tabs. FU [follow up] in one month."

I also track prescriptions, recording where I get them filled, the prescription number, and the cost. This saves time and money should I lose a prescription number or bottle of pills.

Not only is having such information at one's fingertips a convenience; it can also be lifesaving. One woman who attended my seminar and got her life organized around a personal planner returned to class to share her lifesaving story. She and her husband boarded a plane to begin their vacation. Midflight her husband had a heart attack. Because all his medical information was listed in her personal planner that she always carried with her, airline personnel were able to get in touch with his physician, give emergency treatment quickly, and have an ambulance waiting to rush him to the hospital when the plane touched down. With tears in her eyes she publicly credited me and the personal planner idea for saving her husband's life.

Each segment of my life has another priority: I have priorities at work and priorities with the children and priorities in my own life. Keeping all the priorities straight is a constant battle.

Liz Wolff, Teacher

My mother once became very ill while we were visiting her. As she needed immediate medical attention, we transported her to the hospital emergency room, where the attendants plied her with questions. Mother was developing osteoporosis and was in severe pain from what we later learned were stress fractures. Her responses were disconnected and unclear. As I lived 1,000 miles away and knew nothing about her physicians, diagnosis, and medications, I was of little help in providing information.

I had long tried to get Mom motivated to use a personal planner, but she resisted, telling me she didn't want to be bothered at her age. During the next four weeks we spent together while she recuperated, my primary task was to get all her medical information recorded in a personal planner—every physician and medication. Then we began recording every visit to the doctor. Because I lived so far away, I had to be able to track her health records. This information has proved invaluable, as she has a second home in southern California for winter living. Her physician there has to know about diagnosis and treatment from her physician up north. At every visit Mom now records a brief description of the happenings in a source space.

Don't neglect this section of your planner! It can truly mean the difference between life and death.

Household Information

This section includes information needed to run a home, such as mattress sizes and dining room and kitchen table sizes. When I run into a sale on tablecloths, I can buy the right size. I'm a quilter, so I keep samples of fabrics from current quilts there, along with single, double, king, and queen quilt sizes. When redecorating, this is the place to tape fabric and wallpaper samples and paint color chips. It's also the perfect place to keep the size and name of the vacuum cleaner bag, a cleaning formula for washing old quilts, a janitorial supply house where I buy products, and a formula for bleaching my white birdbath each spring.

It is futile to wish for a long life, and then to give so little care to living well.
THOMAS À KEMPIS

I also keep a food budget for an entire year on one page. On one lined page I list each month of the year. I record the totals on a self-stick note each time I spend food dollars during the month. At the end of the month I total these expenditures and record the amount after the month on the food budget page, making it easy to track monthly, as well as yearly, food expenses.

This is also the place I write down the brand names and sizes of clothing family members use. When you shop for new lingerie, record the style and size for shopping convenience the next time you shop.

Sermon Notes and Prayer Requests

Personal planners must also be convenient enough to go to church. You can take notes on the sermon, jotted down on a sheet of lined paper from your planner. (You're sure to get more from the sermon!) Many churches devote time to sharing prayer requests before the congregation. I write them down in my planner, then transfer this page into *My Prayer Notebook,* an organized, elegant method of organizing prayer time. Another page is saved for favorite Bible texts, either to share with a friend or to read when I have a minute.

Besides all the reasons listed above, your planner needs to go to church with you to record events, times, and places. Dinner invitation? Check your calendar and give a nay or yea on the spot. Many times get-togethers or appointments are made in the foyer of the church. Ready access to a planner is a necessity.

Address File

The last section of the planner contains the name, address, and phone number of all personal friends, A-Z, that one would have in a regular address book. Record names permanently in pen, but write addresses and phone numbers in pencil so that changes can be made easily when someone moves.

We had a hearty laugh or two when we were organizing this portion of my mother's address file. As I removed two rubber bands from what was holding her previous two address books together (one containing address information for her northern home, and one for her southern home), dozens of address labels spilled out on the floor, along with miscellaneous scraps of paper. She smiled sheepishly at her habit of tearing address labels from Christmas cards and "filing" them in this manner.

I had scarcely recovered from the shock of such a loosely organized system of tracking addresses, when I began verifying names and addresses of those who would now be entered into her planner. Time after time, when asked about a specific name, she'd say, "Forget that one. He died years ago!" Remember, this section will need to be updated from time to time.

There's also a page for business cards, should you wish to keep them in your planner, and a tablet for notes. This is where I make notes to myself, whenever I'm away from home, regarding any items I must care for upon my return.

In the front of my planner are two file pockets. I use the larger one for a two-year planning calendar, a checkbook, and shopping coupons. In the smaller one I keep self-stick notes, critical for errand and shopping lists. I also keep a running list that may not get tended to for two or more weeks. But when I do get around to it, I won't forget anything, because the list sticks to the inside cover of my planner. On that same page I keep a running list of grocery items needed.

If you purchase the type of planner I recommend, it will last for years. The only additional items ever needed will be a new calendar at the beginning of each year, and additional support for the system should you use all the tabs, source pages, or lined paper. Initially there will be an investment in your planner. Yes, it costs something to get organized. But every penny invested in saving one's sanity is worth it.

My daughter-in-law once asked me to help her get her kitchen organized. (Of course, one never helps a daughter-in-law organize her kitchen unless she asks!) We compiled a list as we assessed what was needed to complete such an organizational task. Then she asked her physician husband (my son) for a couple hundred dollars to purchase the items. My "thrifty" son nearly choked and began giving her the we-can't-afford-it line. Since I was eavesdropping on this conversation, I asked him how efficiently he could run his medical office without proper equipment, say, no exam table, chairs, stethoscope, cotton swabs, or thermometer.

"Got your point, Mom," he quipped as he handed over the cash.

Initially it does cost to get organized. Personal planners do involve a small investment. But a well-designed system will last forever. When at home, keep your personal planner, a pad of self-stick notes, and a pretty pen by the phone you use most frequently.

Never Leave Home Without It

The cardinal rule for using personal planners is: Never leave home without it! When you first begin using a planner, it may be difficult to remember to take it with you as you head out the door. But it soon becomes a habit. You never know when an emergency situation will occur and some bit of information from your planner will be needed. So keep it with you at all times!

Here are a few things your planner can be extended to track:

- a reminder section for doing household chores
- a page to write down gift ideas as they come to mind
- menu plans

- spiritual insights
- weekly "to do" items
- space to record trip information
- a self-check system for developing and evaluating annual or life goals

My initial reaction to being forced to write things down was negative, but it certainly is the answer to Chaos City. A personal planner will assist you in doing the right things, not just the urgent ones. It will help you maintain balance in both your professional and personal lives as you work out your commitments to family, friends, and business associates. With the help of a planner you can do planning for a day, week, month, quarter, year—or your entire life. For further information about how to live happily organized ever after, make a note to purchase a personal planner this week (and don't lose it!).

My personal planner has become the control center of my life. I affectionately call it "My Brain," because it stores information that frees my mind to move on and handle other matters. This is certainly one way to transform a stressed, panicky, bug-eyed bundle of nervous twitching into a devastatingly calm vision of serenity!

> *Dost thou love life?*
> *Then do not squander time,*
> *for that's the stuff*
> *life is made of.*
> BEN FRANKLIN

A Home Control Center

Every business has a base of operations, a place from which management responsibilities are planned and delegated. I consider running an orderly home and family big and important business. Therefore, some type of control center is needed to oversee schedules, appointments, invitations, phone numbers and addresses, and countless other details involved in running a family. Determining an area in your home from which you can manage your family more efficiently will help you as well as your family.

First, choose a convenient location. It might be by the kitchen phone or at a desk in the family room or bedroom. Many new homes are designed with such a center in the kitchen. Perfect for a control center. Other areas you might consider are alcoves, the space under a stairway, a wide landing, a hallway, a foyer, or even a closet.

Next, stock your control center with necessary supplies. These might include:

- a phone (a wall phone frees desk space)
- a bulletin board for messages
- a big calendar on which everyone writes down appointments and activities (if you lack wall space, this can be a large desk blotter)
- a filing cabinet, file box, or drawers for hanging files
- colored file folders
- thumbtacks or push pins
- transparent tape
- a ruler
- rubber bands
- glue
- a stapler
- scissors
- a halogen lamp that can be adjusted to illuminate any area of the desk
- letter trays for filing and organizing papers
- paper clips
- pens, pencils, and markers
- paper and envelopes
- stamps
- self-stick notes
- phone directories
- a calculator

And of course this is the area you will keep your personal planner when you're at home.

Every family member who is old enough becomes responsible for maintaining the control center. Once your control center is set up, hold a family meeting to help each person understand how the control center is to be maintained. Here are some suggestions:

- Each family member is responsible for writing appointments and activities on the calendar. Mom or Dad must know if a ride, gift, or card is needed.
- Phone messages must be posted on the bulletin board, not thrown on top of the desk area.
- Invitations to events are posted on the bulletin board.
- Supplies must be put away after use.
- Each family member will have a file folder, in which important papers are filed.

- Post a cartoon on the bulletin board for fun.
- Everyone assumes responsibility for keeping the control center neat and orderly.

Personalize your space by making it attractive—you'll be more likely to spend time there. Add some desk accessories, such as a pretty lamp, a family photo, or a picture you like.

Let's Use Our Personal Planner

Set It Up:

1. **Purchase your elegant Day Runner Slimline System (or personal planner of your choice).**
2. **Four supplementary items are needed to make your system complete:**
   - slim weekly dated calendar
   - project organizer
   - source pages
   - lined colored paper for sermon notes and prayer requests
3. **Remove the undated calendar from your Day Runner and insert the dated calendar. Place the removable ruler beside today's date.**
4. **Insert five dividers from the project organizer behind the calendar.** Suggested categories are shown at the right. To make a sixth, use a divider labeled "Info" or purchase two project organizers.
5. **Source pages are used behind dividers. In each box on a source page, list information needed for that section.**
6. **Transfer addresses and phone numbers to the address section.** Write names in ink and addresses in pencil so when people move, the address can easily be changed. When you run out of space, as with "S," insert source pages to extend section.
7. **Carry two sizes of self-stick notes in your Day Runner for shopping lists, notes to yourself, and directions to hard-to-find locations.**

**NOW USE AND ENJOY
YOUR NEW
PURSE-SIZED OFFICE!**

Let's Use Our Personal Planner
Label Seven Tabs:

1. PERSONAL
frequently used numbers on one page
family phone numbers, family birthdays
miscellaneous numbers—hair dresser, Amway dealer, neighbors, travel agent, frequently called stores, Avon representative, etc.

2. COMMITTEES
church/women's/social/professional committees

3. BUSINESS

4. ITEMS Lent/THINGS TO REMEMBER
record to whom items lent and date
miscellaneous things to remember
books to purchase
restaurants to try, etc.

5. MEDICAL
phone numbers and addresses of physicians and dentists, personal medical record for self and family—Pap smear, mammogram, prescriptions (number, cost, etc.)
description of family medical problems

6. HOUSEHOLD INFORMATION
mattress, window, table, and room sizes
wallpaper samples, food budget, etc.

7. SERMON NOTES AND PRAYER REQUESTS
date, speaker, main thoughts, text, and prayer requests

**ALWAYS
CARRY IT
WITH YOU!**

Track Appointments and Responsibilities

Assignments:
1. Purchase your personal organizer and get your purse-sized office organized.
2. Create a Home Control Center and stock it with necessary supplies.
3. Design your own business card and have it printed.
4. For personal devotions read Proverbs 16:3: "Commit to the Lord whatever you do, and your plans will succeed" (NIV).

This verse says to me: _____

_____

_____

As a result of what this verse tells me, I will _____

_____

_____

Commit to the Lord whatever
you do, and your plans will succeed.
PROVERBS 16:3, NIV

AFFIRMATION
for Secret to Sanity 3

*T*oday I choose to put order in my life.
Forgetting appointments, over-scheduling myself,
and losing lists and addresses, are behind me. I can
and will get things written down in a personal
planner so I can track appointments and information
successfully. I can develop time-management skills
and use them to become a better person.
It can be done, and it can be fun!

Lift your spirits—go the extra mile

1. Rather than leaving late for an appointment and stressing yourself out, leave a few minutes early and be on time. If you have a few minutes to spare, use the time to collect your thoughts or make notes to yourself. You'll be more poised and more in control for your appointment.
2. Call a busy friend and make a date for lunch to visit, catch up on news, and discuss plans and the progress you've made for getting more order in your life.
3. Make a list of all the things you need to do this week. Once you get this written down, it frees your mind to go on to other things. You'll feel more in control of your time and life.

A big part of preparing meals for a family is creating an emotional, social, and spiritual climate that can assure a successful mealtime experience.

5

SECRET TO SANITY 4:

MENU PLANNING MADE EASY

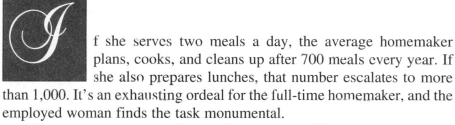

f she serves two meals a day, the average homemaker plans, cooks, and cleans up after 700 meals every year. If she also prepares lunches, that number escalates to more than 1,000. It's an exhausting ordeal for the full-time homemaker, and the employed woman finds the task monumental.

Many women begin suffering from the what'll-we-have-for-supper syndrome about 5:30 every evening. The acute stage of this disease usually hits late afternoon as the victim faces the reality of preparing another meal, although she's probably suffered vague symptoms since finishing supper the night before. She has no ideas, no plans, and few food supplies.

Such families often end up eating out. Not because they want to. Not because eating out was anticipated. Not because they can afford eating out. They eat out because of a lack of planning and organization in the kitchen. Studies show that the average family now eats 3.5 to 4.8 meals away from home each week. The higher the income, the more the family eats out. Because of time constraints and stress, women who are employed full-time eat out more times per week than do homemakers. The average family now spend 36 percent of its food budget on meals eaten away from home.

Eating out is a treat we all should be able to enjoy on occasion. But it costs more money than does eating at home. Furthermore, family interaction and rituals are different, or ignored, when in public. There is more emphasis on manners, more shushing. Families don't talk about the same things when eating out as they do when dining at home. Many may skip saying grace entirely, or may not hold hands during prayer as they might do at home.

When planned for, dining in a restaurant can, and should, be a treat and a reward. We can anticipate it pleasantly when it's on an agenda. But when it is used as an escape from a messy kitchen or one that doesn't contain the proper ingredients for a nutritious meal, or when one is too lazy or unorganized to plan or cook or shop, the reward is missed.

Great events make me quiet and calm; it is only trifles that irritate my nerves.

QUEEN VICTORIA

Unless you can afford to hire a cook of your own, planning menus in advance can save countless hours of mental stewing. Few family managers, whether working full-time or not, have little more than a superficial idea of what meals will be served for an upcoming week. A written menu plan is almost nonexistent in most homes. No wonder many women say they hate to cook.

But how do you plan meals if you've never done it before, if you're used to stopping at the store on the way home from work or simply letting family members fend for themselves?

Step 1: Gain Recipe Control

Researchers have discovered that the average cook uses only 20 percent of her filed recipes, repeating family favorites 80 percent of the time. *This translates into the average cook's preparing about 10 basic dishes, over and over, year in and year out.* Some women have bulging recipe files and still prepare 10 or fewer dishes. Obviously, they would rather "clip" than cook.

In order to menu-plan in an organized manner, all loose recipes must be stored. Gather together all recipes torn from magazines, copied down on scraps of paper, and given to you by friends. Sort this pile into three stacks:

Keepers. This recipe has been tried. It is good and definitely a keeper.

Hope to try someday. This recipe looked good when you tore it from a magazine or tasted it at someone's house. You meant to try it, but haven't yet. It still looks good. You hope to try it some day when you have time.

Never tried, and probably never will be. This recipe is the easiest to handle. Dump it in the wastebasket!

Once the recipes are all sorted, copy the keepers onto recipe cards and get them integrated into your main card file. It would be a questionable use of time to do this for stack two until you know they are keepers. One timesaving idea is to insert these hope-to-try-someday savers into three-hole protector pages and file them in a three-ring binder. Purchase a set of page dividers and label the tabs according to categories: *Beverages, Main Dishes, Veggies, Salads, Desserts,* etc. Your hope-to-try-someday recipes are now orderly. Whenever you have a few spare minutes and want to experiment with something new, your new system can be accessed easily. You have just achieved recipe control.

Step 2: Create a Master Recipe File

Even if you've been cooking, purchasing cookbooks, and collecting recipes for years, menu planning can still be overwhelming without a master file—a collection of favorite family recipes at your fingertips.

First, purchase a pretty three-ring recipe book. If it comes with recipes, toss them. My recipe book was purchased to match my kitchen decor and sits upright on a stand on the kitchen counter for easy accessibility. You will also need three-ring "flip files," which resemble those used for photos, to insert into your recipe book. (Many recipe books come with them.) Additional flip files can be purchased at kitchen stores and stationers where recipe books are sold. I suppose I have 10 flip files in my master file—one for miscellaneous main dishes, another for pasta, and a third for soups, etc., with like dishes grouped together.

Select 20 of your family's favorite main dishes. Why 20? Well, since the average cook repeats only 10 recipes, you can be twice as good by selecting 20! Besides, you're probably already well-acquainted with 10 recipes. Think of family favorites, nutrition, cost, and ease of preparation. If such recipes are already on cards, pull them from your card file. If they're in cookbooks, take a few minutes to copy these favorites onto recipe cards that will fit into your master flip file system.

Once your main dish cards are completed, begin on side dishes. On separate cards, list variations for potatoes (baked, mashed, new boiled potatoes, scalloped, or oven fried). Include several cards for rice (steamed, pilaf, brown). Include at least eight green and yellow vegetable ideas (carrots, asparagus, green peas and onions, green beans with imitation bacon bits, baked acorn squash, spinach).

Add several salad ideas besides a plain tossed green salad. Some suggestions might include coleslaw, cottage cheese and tomatoes on a bed of lettuce, and Caesar, carrot and raisin, fruit, Waldorf, or gelatin salad.

As for desserts, you can plan from zero to a dozen, as it suits you. Most families today attempt to cut down on sweets, saving them for special occasions and weekends.

The assembling of recipes will not seem overwhelming when you consider individual parts of the meal one at a time—entrées, side dishes, vegetables, salads, breads, and desserts. Later you will choose menus from these cards, in mix-and-match fashion, for a week at a time. From these cards will come not only your master menu plan but also your grocery shopping list. Include a card for each recipe, even if you know it from memory. Seeing ingredients listed is helpful when making out grocery lists.

Include cards for even the simplest dishes to prepare. Many women draw a blank when menu planning because they depend on little more than vague recollections from their memory bank. And this task is complicated when you're tired or have nothing in front of you.

I collect and trade pretty blank recipe cards with friends. Then I print my favorite recipes in colored ink, noting from whom I got the recipe. The beautiful card, colored ink, and name of a friend all help to create a pleasant menu-planning experience.

Step 3: Create a Menu Plan

With your menu planner and your elegant and organized recipe book before you, begin sketching menu plans for the next week into the breakfast, lunch, and supper slots on your menu planner. (See Quick and Easy Menu-planning Ideas for Desperate Cooks on page 97.) Include family favorites, but vary your menus from day to day. Being able to glance at the titles of your family's 20 favorites on one page makes this task infinitely easier. Sketch in fruits, vegetables, and desserts as necessary.

As you plan, each category of cards flashes ideas before you. Your cards now become a catalogue of ideas through which you can browse to make choices. As you come across new ideas, add them to your card file, but don't add a card until you have tried it and it has passed the family taste test.

Menu planning can take 10 to 30 minutes or more, depending on your temperament. I'm definitely the 10-minute kind; but my friend Dee is the

60-minute type. Dee subscribes to such magazines as *Bon Appetit* and cherishes each issue, even storing them away for posterity. When I read a printed recipe in a magazine, my taste buds are dead and unresponsive, but Dee studies each recipe with mouth-watering anticipation and experiments with many of them.

Menu planning should be flexible. If you have spaghetti planned for Wednesday night and your husband suggests going out for pizza, please don't insist through clenched teeth that you must follow your menu plan! Since you have all the ingredients on hand, move spaghetti to the next week and be a step ahead on next week's plan.

Save every menu plan for the first six weeks. After that it becomes a breeze to recycle menus, making slight adaptations.

Quick and Easy Meal-planning Ideas for Desperate Cooks

- Have a Crock-Pot night: toss a soup mix into the Crock-Pot before you begin your day. By 5:00 p.m. the smell of simmering soup should be wafting through the house. A fresh salad (from a salad mix, if you prefer) and a tasty bread will complete one easy and nutritious meal.

- Make Friday night special by planning a traditional meal of haystacks or some other family favorite.

- Order take-out food one night a week.

- Have older children and/or your husband plan and prepare a meal one night per week.

- Serve on paper goods for quick cleanup one night a week. No cheap whites, please! They may be economical, but they are flimsy and unattractive. Purchase attractive, colorful paper goods that will bring a smile to your family's face.

- Start a Saturday night food tradition by serving apples and popcorn, or something special your family enjoys.

Step 4: Prepare a Shopping List

Even though you now have some great menu plans in your hot little hands, you still can't prepare meals if the ingredients aren't available. No ingredients, no meals. So after your menu is sketched in on your menu planner, check each recipe's ingredients against the stock you have in your pantry, refrigerator, and freezer. If you see orange juice listed for breakfast, check your current supply. If a recipe calls for canned milk, check your shelves to see the status of canned milk. Write down what is needed on your shopping list.

When planning, keep in mind family preferences and let them dictate, or at least influence, your choices. There may be a terrific sale on cauliflower, but if no one in your family likes cauliflower, this is not a good buy for you at any price. You won't save anything on an item you must throw away.

Impulse buying is the best way to sabotage a food budget. Surveys show you spend 50 cents a minute on impulse buying if you linger in a store more than 30 minutes. So get in there, and get out! Shop with your list in your hand, and there will be fewer decisions to make at the store. Those who rush to the store without a list almost always come home with items that are completely unnecessary. This does not mean that you will never take advantage of in-store bargains you happen on, but unless you have a good reason not to, stick to your list!

If you want something done, ask a busy person.
ANONYMOUS

Menu planning and grocery shopping should be done at the same time every week, if possible. Wednesday and Thursday are the best shopping days, since supermarkets generally begin their sales on Wednesday. You'll battle fewer people at midweek, and sale items will still be in stock. And by then you usually know what your weekend plans will include—dinner with Grandma, church fellowship dinner, or eating out with friends—and can buy accordingly.

Replace items as you run out. Keep a pen and a pad of self-stick notes in the kitchen for jotting down needed items as you notice your supply is getting low to ensure they will be there when you need them. Don't wait until you are totally out, because then you're off to the store on another emergency, time-wasting trip for what begins as one item and ends with three or four impulse buys.

All the effort put into menu planning may have a side benefit you hadn't counted on. It's possible that if your menus are written out and all the ingredients are available, someone else might cook for you! Planning a menu and gathering ingredients is the hardest part. A husband or child might not recognize that tomato sauce, an onion, and noodles—all from different cupboards—spell *lasagna*. Menu planning makes it easier for others to help or even take over completely. If you are sick or must be away from home, menu plans can put your mind at ease and be a great help to the one who assumes your place in the kitchen.

Although most women agree this is a workable plan, few operate this way. The major problem is getting recipes and ideas onto recipe cards so you can make choices in the manner suggested. Unless you have several days of uninterrupted time available, it may take weeks to get this part of your life organized. But keep at it, even if it means doing only two or three recipes at a time. Once you have family favorites on recipe cards and have them assembled in a flip-file book, the menu planning, shopping, and cooking become much, much easier. You'll never again wonder, *What can we have for dinner tonight?* You'll *know* what you are having. No more agonizing.

The Psychology of Shopping.

The average family spends between 17 and 20 percent of net income on food. Approximately one fourth of the food budget includes nonedible sundries, such as paper products, beauty aids, health items, and pet food. Yet these purchases are not included in the 17 to 20 percent. Since a substantial portion of the family budget is spent in a supermarket, careful planning is called for. There is definitely a psychology to becoming an expert shopper. Preparing for a trip to the store can result in tremendous savings.

Shop no more often than once a week. All experts agree that weekly shopping works best. More time and money can be saved by doing major shopping every other week, or even monthly, purchasing only perishable items, such as fresh vegetables or milk, on a weekly basis.

Most markets are arranged strategically to the grocer's advantage. Even if they're buying only bread and milk, shoppers must walk past expensive snacks and gourmet foods. Bread and milk, items people use daily, are almost always placed toward the back of a store. Grocers know that most people simply can't resist the lure of costly impulse items, and will leave the store with something they didn't intend to buy. Smart shopping involves outsmarting the grocers at their own game. Being aware of their strategies helps do this.

Although I am certain that Erma Bombeck would have made a delightful neighbor (great humorist that she was), don't follow her shopping habits. Erma told her neighbors to call her anytime they needed anything at the store, because she went every two hours.

Select the best time of day. Shop when you're on top of things rather than when you're tired or just wanting to get out, preferably early in the morning or late at night, when the stores are nearly deserted. Take your list and make sure you stick to it.

Choose a favorite supermarket. For the most part, it's wiser to shop at one market. Regardless of the good prices offered through sales and coupons, it is a foolish waste of time, energy, and gas to chase from supermarket to supermarket. Just the thought of waiting in line at another checkout counter should be enough to discourage the idea. The belief that you can save by buying some items at one market and other items at another is faulty and saves little, if any, money. Supermarket prices are very competitive. It's ultimately more sensible to check the sale ads at the store where you shop regularly, than to plan menus first, then run here and there to take advantage of specials that fit your menu plans. Select a supermarket you like and stay with it, adjusting your menus to take advantage of the specials they offer.

Plan your checkout strategy. Develop a pattern of shopping for food. Shop first for canned goods that need to be placed at the bottom of the shopping cart. Pick up fresh produce, frozen foods, and bakery items last.

At the checkout counter, group groceries together for easier storage at home—freezer, refrigerator, cupboards, or pantry. Ask to have the groups put in separate bags. The checkout person will happily accommodate such wishes if you have the items organized so as not to hold up the line.

Avoid store psychology. Not only do stores use expert marketing strategies to attract you to their sales, but they have methods of tempting you to buy expensive items. Frequently expensive brands are put at eye level, where most people look first. The unwary shopper will choose that brand without looking further. The cheaper brand, which may be of good quality, might require stooping or stretching. Other marketing techniques lead you to think you are getting a bargain when you aren't. Frequently a display is placed at the end of an aisle with a large sign stating the price. The price may be the standard price, but the manner of display implies a special buy. Buyer, beware!

Shop with a pocket calculator. Although this is strictly an optional step, it lessens the shock of the total bill when checking out. It also allows you to check on the accuracy of the cashier. The *Journal of Retailing* reports that mistakes are made in approximately 20 percent of all checkout transactions. The larger the order, the greater the chance for a mistake.

Another finding: when orders total more than 25 items, the incidence of error escalates to 25 percent. The study showed these errors resulted in equal numbers of overcharges and undercharges, but overcharges totaled twice as much in dollars and cents as undercharges.*

If the cashier is going too fast for you to verify items as they are rung through, request that he or she wait or slow down. If you think an error has been made, ask the cashier to check the price. This procedure will not nominate you for a favorite customer award, but it lessens the chance of being overcharged. Some lazy clerks may guess at prices, given the chance. The *Journal of Retailing* study concludes that those guesses are incorrect about 80 percent of the time.

Today I saved $7 on my grocery bill by questioning an amount rung up through an automated system. When two bags of apples were weighed and rung up, I questioned the price, as it was much higher than I had paid the week before. The clerk checked the sales tape and assured me they were rung up at 80 cents a pound.

"But the sign said 54 cents a pound," I protested.

He checked his book. "You're right," he said.

When asked how an automated system could make such an error, he responded, "The person who put it in made a mistake."

A $7 error on one item in one order! Watch those checkers as they ring things up.

> *On domesticity: "I'm good with kids and decorating, of course, but if the cooking were up to me, we'd all starve in a really cute room."*
> MARY ENGELBREIT

If the lines are long, bear left. Studies show that Americans tend to bear right. You'll have a better chance of getting out sooner by bearing left. The sooner you get out, chances are less that you'll buy something you don't need. Without exception, checkout counters drown customers in racks of breath mints, magazines, candy bars, and a variety of gadgets to look at while you wait in line. Getting through the checkout sooner lessens the chance you'll give in.

Avoid shopping when hungry. Shopping for food requires stamina. And the oft-repeated bit of advice about not shopping when you're hungry is psychologically sound. That's when you're most likely to indulge in impulse buying.

Men in the Kitchen
Many men are making great contributions in the kitchen these days,

and my hat is off to them. But if you work full-time outside the home and are married to a man who has yet to learn how to do more than come to the table when called, it's time to act!

Call a powwow between the two of you. Inform your spouse that you can no longer handle planning and preparing meals every night of the week, and you need help. State this calmly and pleasantly in "I" messages (no blaming, judging, or put-downs). See what suggestions he might offer. If none are forthcoming, explain that you need at least one night a week off, and you want him to take over. Let him know that if he wants to prepare the meal himself and lets you know what ingredients are necessary, you'll purchase them so they'll be handy.

> *Don't fail to make your smile your children's last memory as they depart for school. A ruffled spirit as a send-off puts the time out of joint for the entire day.*
>
> MRS. G. E. JACKSON

If kitchen duty is beyond the realm of possibility for your man, suggest bringing in take-out food or eating out. Have him select which meal he'll be responsible for, then bow out that night. Stay away from the kitchen and busy yourself elsewhere until he calls you to supper. No complaints, please; only compliments. Remember how long it took you to learn.

Kids in the Kitchen

A survey of working mothers shows that 77 percent prepare dinner alone, and 64 percent handle cleanup alone. This probably occurs because mothers can do it faster than children. It is also easier to do it alone than to stand firm and/or nag the kids to do it. However, these are probably the same moms who complain they don't have enough time with their kids.

Children need to be involved in menu planning, food preparation, and kitchen cleanup. This is a great time for parent and child to work side by side. "You fix the salad while I make the chili." "You set the table while I prepare the vegetable." "You put the dishes in the dishwasher while I put the food away." At ages 4, 5, and 6 children can set the table. Teach them that the fork goes to the left of the plate, the knife to the right with the blade turned in, and the spoon beside it. Teach them to place the glass at the tip of the knife, and the napkin, folded neatly, under the fork. Children can also clear the table, rinse dishes, and load the dishwasher.

They can spray-wipe the table, straighten chairs, sweep the floor, scrub pots and pans, and put food away. They can empty trash, carry in groceries, restock shelves, and carry food to the freezer. By age 8 they should be assisting with meal preparation and by age 9 preparing simple meals on their own.

If you work with your children and turn kitchen duty into a pleasant experience of talking, sharing, and working, they'll look forward to time with Mom in the kitchen. If, however, they are left to bicker among themselves while you bark out orders from another room like a drill sergeant, kitchen duty will be dreaded.

Encourage your children to cook age-appropriate recipes. As soon as they are old enough to take responsibility for making a meal, have them do so. From the time they are 7 or so they can, and should, be making their own lunches, even their own sandwiches.

Have each child master one specialty or meal that no one else in the family can prepare. In our family, Carlene loved to make cakes and decorate them. Omelettes became Rodney's specialty. He became very creative in spawning new versions, often inviting his friends over to enjoy a meal while I stood by and watched. Mark could make a mean batch of chocolate-chip cookies. All three got recognition and praise for turning out their specialty.

"A Happy Meal, Please"
(But Not the Type Obtained at McDonald's)

Meal preparation goes far beyond getting food on the table. Perhaps the most important ingredient at any table is a happy and relaxed wife and mother. It's not only *what* we eat but *how* we eat together that contributes to good nutrition. Our families don't need nutritional experts or gourmet cooks nearly as much as they need women who are available to nurture.

A friend stopped me in a bookstore recently. When she told me how tired she was, I suggested that she might benefit from my seminar on organizing time. As I explained Menu Planning Made Easy, she wearily exclaimed, "I'm so exhausted when I get home I don't care what kind of slop I throw in my kids' mouths."

Many women today might echo her sentiments. The most attractive and well-balanced meal loses value when thought of as "slop" or when served in the midst of bickering, scolding, or disharmony. A big part of preparing meals for a family is creating an emotional, social, and spiritual climate that can assure a successful mealtime experience. I am convinced that mealtime is key to successful family togetherness. The processes of menu planning, food preparation, and eating together are activities that can turn fathers, mothers, and children into loving families.

Avoid making a big deal over food likes and dislikes. Attention to food dislikes sets up super-bad feelings and attitudes toward eating together. If a certain food has not been eaten by the end of a normal mealtime (20 to 30 minutes), remove the plate without comment. One rule can help encourage family members to eat what is served: Those who refuse to eat their meals are never served dessert. Another ironclad rule follows: Never give that child a snack later because of hunger. Let natural consequences take over (in this case hunger), and he or she will be more willing to eat what is served at mealtime.

Sit down with your children when they eat. It is so tempting to seat the family, then go about your business. This is particularly true at breakfast and lunchtime, when all family members may not be present. But precious sharing time can be lost. Your daughters learn that women do not sit with families during the mealtime, and they too will place a low priority on this as they grow up and establish homes of their own. Your sons learn not to expect their wives to join them for a meal. Demonstrate to your family that you consider mealtime an important event. Enjoy the meal with them. Smile. Relax. Enter into their conversations. Encourage someone else in the family to wait on individual needs. You are not the family's servant.

Breakfast Time

It's so easy to let breakfast slide into a dull routine or a time of rushing rudely about. If you aren't a morning person, it may be difficult to apply your best efforts to anything at that time of the day—especially when preparing to rush off to work. Why not encourage the children to plan and prepare their own breakfast one morning a week?

Breakfast is of prime importance. One third of the recommended nutrients for a day should come at breakfast, and the families need the best send-off you can possibly give them. Strive for a variety of nutritious foods. Just as breakfast sets the tone for our physical day, so prayer sets the spiritual tone of our day. And what a perfect time for the whole family to gain spiritual food for the day! Perhaps the children can be encouraged to share a challenge they might face during the day—a test, a difficult friendship, a teacher situation, a ball game. A short prayer offered in earnestness sends the child off with greater assurance. This custom fortifies the family for the challenges of the day and teaches children to rely on God for strength and stability. Don't be surprised if you get reports during the supper hour on prayers answered during the day.

For Ordinary to Appealing Meals

The manner in which you serve your family their daily meals becomes important. Think about *how* you are serving your family, and *where*—the kitchen table, the dining room, a breakfast bar. You may work full-time outside the home and come home exhausted. Just getting food on the table may be your main goal. But the atmosphere in which your family consumes the food is almost as important as the nutrients in the food. It's what is called *ambience.*

We expect ambience when we eat at a French or Italian restaurant. But ambience can, and should, be attained at home too. And it doesn't have to be time-consuming, nor is it beyond the abilities of a stressed and frazzled mom. Ambience can be added quickly and easily by lighting a candle, using goblets rather than everyday glassware, placing a lemon wedge over the edge of a glass, displaying a bouquet of fresh flowers, playing dinner music, sprinkling oregano over pasta, or serving spaghetti from a silver platter rather than straight from the pot on the stove. Little touches like this add panache to common, everyday rituals and turn ordinary events into memorable occasions.

> *Eating together . . . peppered with aesthetic and aromatic touches, . . . can make meals and family time more memorable.*
>
> KATHY PEAL, "PLEASE PASS THE AMBIANCE," IN *ASPIRE*

Give some thoughts to how you might make your table practical but attractive. A top-quality vinyl cloth can add color and interest to everyday table settings. They can become an attractive part of the room's decor at the same time they're protecting the surface of the table and making a good work surface for small projects or study.

Cloth napkins made of stain-repellent, durable-press fabrics can add pizzazz and color to a table setting. A fresh one folded or presented with a napkin ring at each place setting for each family member once or twice a week doesn't add much to the laundry. You'll make the meal more memorable and foster family unity.

Eating together cultivates closeness. Presentation transforms the ordinary into appealing. Eating together as a family is a lost art, a last frontier.

Making Fridays Special

Sometimes it's nice to turn a regular meal into a special occasion. We always tried to make dinner a time for happy discussions, but Friday night was designated as really special. The table was set with special mats and a different set of dishes than those used the rest of the week. The simple menu was always the same: in winter, soup and muffins with grape juice; in summer, haystacks and grape juice, with ice cream for dessert.

A lighted candle glowed from the center of the table. And sometimes we even dressed up. While soft music played in the background, we held hands during prayer, then told about one special thing that had happened during the week.

> *Christ is the Head of this house, the unseen Guest at every meal, the silent Listener to every conversation.*
>
> ELLEN WHITE

After supper I did a quick cleanup of the kitchen, and the kids gathered for family night. We enjoyed such varied activities as guessing games, pantomimes, musicals, and dramas. Perhaps the most fun of all were the Bible stories acted out by the three children. Carlene directed (because she was the oldest and the bossiest), Rodney obeyed willingly (because he was the most adaptable), and Mark dragged his feet (because he could). Their reenactments included writing scripts and raiding the linen and clothes closets for props.

Then we would sit around a crackling fire (in the wintertime) and read aloud. Sometimes we took turns reading, but together we explored many books that provided spiritual lessons and direction to our lives. Repetition cemented this practice into a family tradition. Now that our children have homes of their own, they too follow the practice of making Friday night special. No television, jobs, school, or extracurricular activities were allowed to invade this time, which became almost hallowed to our family.

Create your own special family night. Encourage the children to sing, play the piano, recite a poem, or act out a charade. They can do things alone, in pairs, or involve the entire family. Close the evening by praying together. Our custom was to kneel in a circle with our arms around each other, symbolizing the unbroken circle of love that has held us all together over the years. Children cherish traditions and draw security from them. Traditions tell them there are things in life that are unchanging, but they can always be counted on.

From Tired Meal to Happy Meals

By now you may have discovered that once you became a wife and mother, you did not automatically become someone who delighted in serving "happy homemaker" meals. It is difficult to meet a never-ending schedule of three meals a day, whether you feel like it or not. Nevertheless, like it or not, most of the menu planning falls on our shoulders. I do not relish menu planning, grocery shopping, or meal planning preparation. I prefer cooking meals for company, when I get some adulation for my efforts! So menu planning had to become a commitment for me, and I find I must continually recommit my energy and intentions to the process. Occasionally I reward myself by taking a night off or by ordering take-out food. And Harry sometimes rewards me by offering to take me out to eat. These brief respites amid the daily grind of preparing two to three meals every day are a necessity.

If you've been serving "tired meals" to a family who is tired of them you can regain enthusiasm for this task once again. If you are not really a good cook, you can become one. The busier you are, and the less time you have to cook, the more necessary it is for you to master this secret to sanity. You don't have time for disasters or for blindly muddling through recipes you're not certain about.

If you are not really a good cook, you can become one. The busier you are, and the less time you have to cook, the more necessary it is for you to master this secret to sanity.

Good cooking takes no more time than bad cooking. Meal planning and preparation can be reduced to a relatively simple task once you have recipe control, have the ingredients on hand, and have a menu plan. Time spent in mastering this secret to sanity is one of the wisest investments a family manager can make. Besides saving time and money, it provides much family enjoyment. Good nutritious meals satisfy more than hunger. Eaten together as a family with enjoyment, meals can be a pleasant experience that will be remembered for all the years to come.

---

*Joan Bingham, *Smart Shopper's Guide to Food Buying and Preparation* (New York: Scribner's, 1982), p. 71.

Time Savers to Get You Out of the Kitchen Fast

- Save freezer space and time by baking certain casseroles in a baking dish that's lined with heavy freezer foil. Freeze the casserole, then slide it out of its container, slip it into a plastic bag, and return it to the freezer. When ready to use, remove the foil and set the contents back into the container.

- Buy prepared foods. They cost a little more, but prewashed salad mix, grated cheese, and peeled carrots all cut down on preparation time and mess.

- Cut down on the number of dishes used in food preparation. Mix the salad dressing in the same bowl from which you serve the salad. Grate carrots on waxed paper or a paper towel that can be tossed, rather than a plate that must be washed.

- Use freezer-to-oven-to-table cookware.

- Assemble all ingredients before beginning to cook. This spares you the aggravation of getting halfway through a recipe before realizing a key ingredient is missing.

- Limit grocery shopping to one or two stores. You can speed through the aisles because you know the layout, and you can track sale items easily.

- Keep your pantry stocked with basic food items you use regularly. This cuts down on last-minute treks to the store.

- Learn to improve. If a recipe calls for an ingredient you don't have, substitute something you do have. Great recipes have been born out of creative necessity!

- Want to reduce the times you have to wash utensils? Measure dry ingredients before wet ones. Measure flour before milk. When using a food processor, chop dry ingredients first, then wet ones.

- Prepare double batches of recipes, and freeze half for a future meal.

- Place your cutting board over the edge of the sink with a disposal. You can slide cut foods directly into a dish or pot, or into the disposal.

- Cover the countertop with waxed paper to catch crumbs or spills. Cleanup is a breeze—simply roll up the paper and discard.

- Line baking pans with aluminum foil to avoid the need to scrub later.

- To avoid sticky hands and knives, keep jelly or honey in a plastic squeeze bottle.

- Place a trash container on the floor near your work area, where wrappers, cans, and containers can be tossed immediately.

- If something spills on the oven floor while baking, immediately sprinkle salt on the spill. When the oven is cool, wipe up the salt with a cloth.

- Place a paper plate or paper towel between pots and pans to keep them from becoming scratched.

- Have a specific place for everything. If you (and your family) know where utensils belong, you won't waste time looking for them.

- Store equipment and food near the place where they will be used. For example, keep the mixing bowls and flour sifter near the baking center.

- Reduce cupboard clutter to only what is necessary. If there are only three of you in the family, you probably don't need a 20-piece dish set. Store what isn't necessary.

WEEKLY MENU PLANNER

Date _____

Days	Breakfast	Lunch	Dinner
Thursday			
Friday			
Saturday			
Sunday			
Monday			
Tuesday			
Wednesday			

Shopping List:

_____	_____	_____
_____	_____	_____
_____	_____	_____
_____	_____	_____
_____	_____	_____
_____	_____	_____

Menu Planning Made Easy

Assignments:
1. Sit down with your menu planner; sketch in menu plans for the up-coming week. During personal time sort through recipes, discarding the never-tried-and-probably-never-will-be pile. Copy 20 family favorites on pretty recipe cards and get them organized in a flip-file recipe book. This won't get meals on the table—but getting this far makes it infinitely easier.
2. For personal devotions read Ecclesiastes 9:10: "Whatever your hand finds to do, do it with all your might" (NIV).

This verse says to me: _____

_____

_____

As a result of what this verse tells me, I will _____

_____

_____

*The best way to get a good start
in the morning is to get a
good night's sleep the night before.*

AFFIRMATION
for Secret to Sanity 4

*T*oday I choose to put order in my life.
I can and will make menu planning
a priority this week to lessen my stress level. I will
also begin to sort through recipe clutter
and gain control over this area of my life.
It can be done, and it can be fun!

Lift your spirits—go the extra mile

1. Bring color to the heart of your home. Purchase a small pot of flowers. Put them in a basket to adorn your kitchen table for daily appreciation of God's creation and beauty—or to make Friday special.
2. Bake some chocolate-chip cookies and leave them to cool on cookie racks. Nothing says "home" faster than the smell of home-baked cookies. Think of sharing a few with a neighbor, a friend, or a shut-in.
3. Prepare a "love basket" for someone you care about. Line a basket with a pretty tea towel. Fill the basket with tea and sweets, a sandwich, or a pot of soup. Decorate the handle with a bow. Deliver the basket in person.
4. Add a little fun and specialness to a family meal this week. Eat by candlelight, use a place mat or different set of dishes. Look for new ways in which you can turn an ordinary meal into a memorable experience.

*Closets must delight your eye when you open the door.
Closet space can be decorated with paint, wallpaper, or posters.*

6

SECRET TO SANITY 5:

HOW TO SORT THROUGH THE CLUTTER

ost people cannot live without their "stuff." In fact, they rent (or buy) living space just to store it. When they run out of living space, they go to see Derrel, the guy who owns all those ministorage places and is making a mint off people who run out of space to store their stuff at home. One man told me he had paid out $10,000 in the past couple years to house things his wife refuses to part with!

How about you? If I were to visit your home and check out your drawers, cupboards, and closets, how many of the following items would I find?

- Watches that no longer run.
- Craft projects begun but never finished.
- Stacks of expired coupons for products you never buy.
- Broken tools and toys.
- Outdated medications.
- Abandoned bottles of makeup.
- Scraps of soap.
- Draperies and bedspreads from a former house.

- Books you've never finished reading.
- Pots from all the plants that died.
- Boxes of unread magazines that you plan to go through someday.
- An unopened pregnancy kit—even though it's been three years since your last period.

Why do we keep all this stuff? We have a million excuses:

I might need it someday. Good excuse. But did you know it's much easier to buy a new screw than to pick through a container of nails, tacks, pushpins, picture hangers, and other rusty and sharp objects you've saved for decades?

It's been in the family for years. If you saved every token of meaningful stuff from your family, you'd soon be living in a warehouse.

I'll get around to fixing it sometime. Only 2 percent of all broken things ever get fixed. (Unless you're married to Harry Van Pelt. He can fix almost any broken item, because he has every tool that's ever been invented. Guess what kind of clutter problem *this* creates.)

It's still perfectly good. Apply the two-year rule: If you haven't used it in two years, chances are 100 to 1 that you never will. Get rid of it.

> *With my invitations I send directions as a guide, but my house is such a mess they need a map for the inside.*
>
> PHYLLIS DILLER

A New Addiction

Clutter addicts who want to save it all suffer from a grave emotional disease called house blindness. Science can't explain it, but the symptoms are clear. The sufferer grows blind to clutter. Clutter becomes a way of life. The major symptom is that stuff left somewhere for three days stays there forever. Why? Because it is no longer seen. Some cases are particularly severe. The patient no longer sees the cesspool of junk mail on the table. Or the filthy sheet thrown over the couch to protect it from where the dog slept. (The dog died four months ago.)

What about the ant farm Brad got for Christmas? The last ant gave up a year ago, and now dead ants are displayed on top of the television. Or the baby seat dangling in the doorway? Your youngster hasn't used it in two years. You still shove it aside every time you go through the doorway, but you're used to it now. It's January, and the ugly old fan used last summer is still in the living room.

So Much Stuff!

A normal household has more than 3,500 items in it, but we use fewer than 15 percent of them. Some of these items may come in handy from time to time, but most of the time they do little more than gather dust and get in our way.

It's been estimated that one third of everything we own falls into the "clutter" category. Nowadays the average American family moves 14 times in a lifetime. So if a third of your stuff constitutes clutter, you could save the effort of loading eight moving vans by decluttering before moving! People spend literally thousands of hard-earned dollars by shuffling clutter around the country.

My sister discovered this the day she moved from northern California to Washington State. Here's an excerpt from her letter:

Sunday was loading day. Dudley and six strong friends had the truck all loaded in only a few hours. Even though we rented the largest Ryder truck, we weren't sure we could get everything in, but the guys did a fantastic job of packing. Using every possible square inch, we eventually made it. There was hardly room for a toothpick to be squeezed in before the door was closed. (I've made four trips to Washington in the past few months, each time bringing a load. It's a good thing I did, or we wouldn't have gotten everything in the truck.) We also loaded the pickup full and towed it behind the Ryder truck. I drove our motor home (fully packed).

Why, oh, why do we Americans have so much "stuff"? Here's my advice: If you can possibly live without it, don't buy it, because you will have to move it some day, and then you'll wish you didn't have it!

My daughter, who is a real collector of things, made the same discovery when she decluttered prior to a recent move to Florida. Even though she held a couple garage sales to prune down the clutter, there were still piles left. Her husband had to rent a truck to haul it away ($100) to a disposal site, where their junk weighed in at 2,200 pounds ($89). Counting what it cost to fill the gas tank ($20), the total cost to get rid of it all was $209.

The point is, don't collect it in the first place. Think about what's cluttering your home right now. It's highly probable that you're harboring a bunch of useless stuff. And once you have it, you have to store it. And feel obligated to use it. Sometimes you become sentimentally attached to it. And you *never* have time to go back and sort through all of it.

The Negative Effect of Clutter

Clutter affects us negatively in many ways.

Clutter robs us of time. We spend a valuable portion of our time polishing, dusting, cleaning, and moving it around.

Clutter costs money. When shopping, remember: When you get that item home, you have to put it someplace. Ask yourself: *Do I really need this? Might the money be spent better elsewhere?* We really can't afford to clutter our lives!

A cluttered house takes more time and effort to clean.

A cluttered house affects our relationship with our family. Many families want to be closer but can't be, because of clutter. Clutter separates them from one another. A man spoke out on this point at one of my seminars.

"Nancy," he said, flashing a dimpled grin, "you say that men should romance their wives. I want to romance my wife, but I'll have to find her first! She's almost buried in clutter!"

I wouldn't even venture an estimate regarding the number of marital arguments that focus on clutter and disorganization.

Solutions to Clutter

Yes, many people are in bondage to clutter. If you have a clutter problem, here are some solutions:

You can move to a smaller home. You'll get rid of clutter by necessity. Friends of mine moved to an apartment while a larger home was being built. Most of their things were in storage while they lived with only bare essentials for a few months. The wife said she enjoyed the experience, because living was so carefree. Think about it!

You could have all your clutter cremated. Then take the ashes and place them in a lovely urn and display it on the mantle. This way it can always be with you, even though in condensed form.

You can take pictures of it. Take multiple pictures of all the clutter you have on display. Don't forget all the hidden clutter in drawers and closets. Mount your collection of photographs in an album and display the album on the coffee table—then toss the clutter.

Are you convinced yet that you need to sort through the clutter in your home? OK. Here's one more reason. It's scriptural.

> "There is a time for everything,
>   and a season for every activity under heaven:
>   a time to be born and a time to die,

a time to plant and a time to uproot,
a time to kill and a time to heal,
a time to tear down and a time to build,
a time to weep and a time to laugh,
a time to mourn and a time to dance,
a time to scatter stones and a time to gather them,
a time to embrace and a time to refrain,
a time to search and a time to give up,
a time to keep and a time to throw away."
—Ecclesiastes 3:1-6, NIV

So there you have it. The time has come to throw away . . . or at least sort through.

The First Challenge: Surface Clutter

It isn't enough to talk about clutter problems. It's easier to tackle the problem when you have a defined plan. So here's the Declutter Plan:

Begin at the front door. Go to your front door. Turn around and face your house as if you were entering. The first room on your left is where to begin—unless it's your kitchen. (Kitchens are major clutter problems, so we'll get to the kitchen later, when we're experienced.) Proceed in clockwise fashion through your home, decluttering every room, closet, cupboard, and drawer as you proceed, until you arrive back at the front door. Do the same with upstairs, basement, and garage areas, always working clockwise from the main entrance.

> *Removing clutter prepares us mentally and our home physically to make way for the new, and to improve our surroundings.*
>
> ALEXANDRA STODDARD

Label four containers. Take four containers with you (boxes or garbage bags). Label one "Throw Away." Empty this one often, before suffering separation anxiety or a change of mind. Label the second one "Give Away or Sell." The third one is the "Put Away" container. And the last one is labeled "Store."

Work from the outside in. Clear visible clutter before going after clutter in drawers, cupboards, or closets. Everything that needs to be put away goes into the "Put Away" container. Clear out anything that doesn't belong in that room—stacks of paper, boxes, piles of magazines, and miscellaneous items. If you drag hidden clutter out of drawers and cupboards first, it will make a double mess and complicate decisions about whether to throw away, sell/give away, put away, or store. Then you'll likely get discouraged and quit.

When you're finished, give the room THE TEST.

THE TEST for Living Rooms, Dining Rooms, and Family Rooms (Dens and Studies, Too)

Walls. Study your walls. If you've lived in your house for several years, you may find more and more things hanging, dangling, or suspended from your walls. Too much is too much and gives a room a cluttered appearance. When I gave my rooms THE TEST, I knew immediately I was in big trouble. Country decorating can be fun, but it can get overdone very quickly. I had a country wreath and a wall grouping over the fireplace that included a shelf, hanging candles, little houses, a wooden plaque, and another wreath. Pure clutter! I simplified to one item on the wall. Check your walls to see what should stay for aesthetic purposes, and what gives a messy appearance.

Windowsills. Nothing clutters an area faster than knickknacks adorning windowsills. Perfume bottles, figurines, collector's items, and sprouting plants all look messy and obstruct the view. On dusting day each item must be lifted and cleaned. An uncluttered windowsill gives a room a better look and simplifies cleaning.

Furniture. Next, evaluate the pieces of furniture in the room. Are there big and little tables everywhere—against the walls, next to the sofa, and beside the bed? Too many tables take up room and collect clutter. Which tables are necessary? Can any be eliminated? Do the same with sofas, chairs, and lamps.

Books, magazines, and newspapers. Most people display too many books. More than 55,000 new books are published every year (more than 1,000 a week). Read and enjoy your books. Learn from your books. Then pass them on to someone else who can benefit from them. Don't hold on to outdated information. Books kept should be judged by their reference value.

Collections. Collections of anything—be it baseball cards, coins, teddy bears, salt and pepper shakers, or rocks—become major clutter problems and can be hazardous to your organizational health. Whether these collections are stored in the house or in the garage, in full view or in cupboards or boxes, they require care when space is needed for something else. Evaluate how much time you want to spend dusting, cleaning, and maintaining your collection. If you can't bear to part with it, keep a few choice selections and sell or give away the rest. If you have children who are shifting into the collector's mode, set limits now before it gets out of hand. Teach them early in life about the value of organization and utilization of space and how to prioritize the accumulation of things in their lives. If you or a family member do have a collection, keep it confined to a specific area, display case, or cabinet.

Now, critically examine everything left in the room. Each item should have a valid reason for being there, whether it's for function or looks. Countertops or tables with too much stuff, even if it's pretty, make a room look messy. Cleared surfaces give a room an immediate sense of order.

If there's an antique clock on the table that doesn't work, it may still be attractive. So it passes THE TEST. But if it's ugly and no longer works and the only reason you're keeping it there is that Grandma might notice it's gone, it doesn't pass THE TEST.

Scrutinize each room and every table, end table, nightstand, mantel, shelf, drawer, and wall in that room. Make a decision as you remove each item: throw away, give away or sell, put away, or store. If you aren't sure about some things, store them in a box marked "Undecided" for a month. But get them out of sight. If you never miss them, or if you like the room without them, get rid of them.

The Second Challenge: Hidden Clutter

The first step in decluttering is to "see" surface clutter and eliminate it. This second, more advanced step is to eliminate hidden clutter that lurks in drawers, cupboards, and closets. Although I've never been a clutter addict, I have experienced a sense of pride and accomplishment once I gave each room THE TEST and further simplified my home. But this was nothing compared to how I felt after ridding my home of *hidden* clutter.

I didn't have the courage to tackle this alone, so I awaited a visit from my daughter. With Carlene's encouragement and quick decision-making ability about whether to toss or save, all 20 drawers in the bedroom were soon neat, organized, and pretty. Getting rid of stashed stuff is almost a spiritual experience, like finally forgiving someone who hurt you long ago. With clean drawers and cupboards came a new sense of cleanliness and organization. I was free! It felt good.

Although drawers, cupboards, and closets must be maintained to stay organized, maintenance is much simpler after the first major clearing out. I can quickly restore order by spending a minute or two per drawer or cupboard.

Here's a suggested plan for tackling the hidden clutter:

1. *Empty the contents of drawers/cupboards onto a plastic tablecloth.* If there's nothing breakable in the drawer, tip it upside down. In other words, take *everything* out.

2. *Clean the drawer, cupboard, or shelf.* Wipe the area with a cleaning cloth that's been dampened with an all-purpose cleaner.

3. *Replace the drawer's lining.* Most drawers need some type of lining—attractive, colorful, and elegant, or contact paper in colors that delight you. Whenever you wallpaper a room, save scraps as lining for drawers. Or paint. A good painted surface is easier to clean and straighten than fooling with shelf paper.

Now you are ready for THE TEST: Bedrooms and Bathrooms.

THE TEST for Bedrooms and Bathrooms

Bedrooms. Study each wall, counter, dresser, and nightstand. Is there clutter that needs to be disposed of? Are there piles of mail, books, drinking glasses, newspapers, perfume bottles, or pill bottles piled on, or cluttering, any surface? (We'll talk about decluttering children's bedrooms later.)

Bathrooms. Solve the number one bathroom problem: countertop clutter. Gather all perfumes, combs, mousses, toothbrushes, plants, and seashells and organize them into baskets, grouping like things together, and store them out of sight. Now choose two or three important and attractive items to set on the counter. Toss the rest. Your counter space can now be cleaned in half the time.

Get rid of tank and toilet seat covers. They collect dust, germs, and odor and must be removed and washed and put back on again. It's easier to clean a toilet without them. Besides, toilets don't need them—they don't catch cold!

Peek behind the shower door. How many bottles, jars, soap scraps, toys, and other bath (and nonbath) items clutter the floor and walls? Install a two-tiered shelf (more if necessary) in an easy-reach area. Keep everything needed for baths there.

Check out your bathroom drawers. Are they crammed with squeezed-out tubes, half-empty jars, and makeup all in the wrong shades? Are samples of this and that all jumbled together in a bed of loose hair and spilled face powder? Dump everything out on a plastic cloth. Wipe—or scrub—the drawer, then line it with attractive contact paper to match the colors and decor of your bathroom. Purchase plastic drawer dividers with movable sections for grouping like things together. Toss outdated cosmetics and toiletries. Put back into this drawer only what belongs! Toothbrushes, paste, and floss can go in one tray; hairbrushes and combs in another. Group makeup in the same manner.

Travel supplies. Store all travel items, such as hair dryer, iron, curling iron, and adapters, in one basket so they are all together and ready to travel when you are.

Hair products. It's easy to retrieve the hair product you want when you want it if you group like things together in small baskets with labels on the front. Put shampoos and conditioners in one; hair sprays, foams, and gels in another; and hair color in a third. Store curling irons and blow driers in a wicker wastebasket in a handy spot on the floor. Home permanent supplies, hot rollers, and other supplies not used frequently can go on a lower shelf behind the baskets containing supplies used regularly.

Medicines. Medicine shelves are often the home of forgotten stuff. Segregate prescription medications from first-aid supplies. Put them in plastic baskets and label them. Store this in a safe area, out of reach of children. Baskets serve as minidrawers that can be pulled out and shoved back in. No more getting down on your hands and knees and blindly groping for what you need from a collection of stuff. Check every prescription bottle, discarding what is outdated. (Outdated medications should be flushed down the toilet, not dumped in the trash, where they could endanger someone's life.)

4. Put back into the drawer or cupboard only what belongs there, grouping like things together. Where you currently keep things may not be the best or most efficient location. Begin by grouping. Place sewing supplies in a specific drawer, closest to where they are needed. Store art and crafts projects in boxes on specific shelves. Do the same with photos, tools, books, toys, stationery, and mending.

5. *Make a list of needed supplies.* As you sort, group, and organize, you may notice missing supplies (Band-Aids, candles, napkins, cleansers, doormats) or needed repairs. Jot them down on a pad of self-stick notes. At the end of your declutter shift, put this list in your daily planner book. You can pick the supplies up the next time you make a trip to town.

6. *Make decisions to throw away, give away or sell, put away, or store.* As you finish your sorting shift for the day, or as you complete each room, make a decision regarding what to do with the bags/boxes you have collected. Get the **throwaway** items to the garbage can immediately. Take the **put-away** items to their rightful places. Prepare a storage area in the basement or garage for your **giveaway** or yard sale items.

7. *Complete one room each week.* This means that if you live in a six-room house and are a full-time homemaker, you can have things under control in six weeks. If you are an employed person, you'll likely need double that time. It doesn't matter how long it takes. What matters is that you have a plan for decluttering your home, and that you are getting it done, even if gradually.

8. *Do the kitchen last.* Kitchens are major declutter projects. Tackle this room only after you've first gained experience in other rooms. Knowing what you are doing raises your confidence level. Starting at the kitchen sink, work clockwise around the room. Group like things together. Think through what you need to have handy and the number of steps required to reach these items.

If you need more help, get a book from the library on kitchen organization.

Now you're ready for THE TEST: Kitchens.

THE TEST for Kitchens

Appliances. In a quest for laborsaving devices, we frequently clutter the kitchen with can openers, warmers, blenders, electrical gadgets, Crock-Pots, popcorn poppers, pasta makers, coffeemakers, french fry cutters, food processors, grinders, and deep-fat fryers that we rarely or never use. Most kitchens have little enough counter space and even less cupboard space to accommodate storage. Portable kitchen centers can be purchased to provide extra countertop work space, as well as storage underneath.

But the best way to handle the plethora of appliances is to get rid of what is not used on a regular basis. If it is stored in the back of a shelf and too much trouble to get out and put away again, or if it has so many parts that you don't know how to use it, get rid of it. And dump broken appliances—only 2 percent are ever repaired.

Simplify. Dump contraptions that have become dust collectors. Put unneeded and broken items in the Sell or Give Away box. Clear that kitchen counter, and it will instantly become easier to keep clean.

Pots and pans. Pots and pans usually end up being stacked in unmanageable heaps. Getting to the one you want involves bending over and unloading all the pans set inside the one you want. Then you must replace the pots you just lifted out. The whole process must be repeated to put it back. No wonder cooks get cranky!

Get rid of all the old pots and pans you've kept since your wedding day (unless you were married last month). Ditto for the fancy gourmet pans and molds you never use. If you do use them once a year, store them in one of those unreachable spaces, such as the cupboard over the refrigerator.

Regardless of what kind of cook you are, having ready access to pots and pans that are arranged in an orderly manner reduces aggravation—and cleanup is easier and faster. Organizing even this much of your kitchen could easily put a little joy back into cooking.

Plastic food containers. Dump all the butter and cottage cheese containers that currently litter your cupboards! Treat yourself to a matching set of see-through, stackable plastic containers. Store all the lids to your set in one small plastic basket. See the difference this one change makes in your cupboards.

Kitchen utensils. Peek inside your utensil drawers (proceed with caution—they multiply even while you watch!). Look at the proliferation of spatulas, bottle openers, wooden spoons (some broken), pastry cutters, eggbeaters, corn-on-the-cob holders, pancake turners, can openers, and dozens of whatchamacallits and thingamajigs. Another drawer probably contains duplicates of graters, strainers, funnels, and sifters, not to mention unidentifiable doodads and parts you think belong to the appliances you just got rid of. Don't forget to count the crocks of utensils standing upright on the stove.

First of all, get rid of unnecessary duplicates. Next, toss those gourmet gadgets you never use. Toss the unidentifiable doodads and parts. Inventory what needs to be replaced. (Why is it women will buy a new dress but resist purchasing a new spatula when necessary?) Go through flatware in the same manner, weeding out mismatched pieces and nonessentials. Store what's left in cutlery trays specially made for this purpose. Some people will try to get you to stick these things in a ceramic jar or hang them from hooks on pegs. This creates a cluttered appearance and takes away counter space. Besides, each time you clean, the ceramic jar must be cleaned, lifted, and cleaned under. The simpler you keep your kitchen space, the easier it is to clean. Resist gadgets!

Cookbook clutter. Rule of thumb: You can keep any cookbook containing five recipes you use regularly. If it contains fewer than five, copy the ones you use and give the book away. Keep five of your favorite cookbooks—10 if you are a gourmet cook.

Dishes. Most people have enough dishes stashed behind cupboard doors to serve an army on. You'll likely find several sets of everyday dishes, wedding dishes, inherited dishes, heirloom dishes, promotional dishes, and souvenir dishes. Now count the pieces of assorted glassware and mugs cluttering your shelves. If you can't count that high, it's time to weed out.

You'll need an everyday dish set. If you rarely use the cups and saucers and other pieces that came with the set, store them in one of those unreachable spots. Buy yourself a set or two of matching everyday glasses and get rid of all the mismatched glasses you've collected over the years.

Good china becomes a storage problem, especially if you are from a family such as mine. My mother has given me two sets of dishes for entertaining (one an irreplaceable heirloom set from Hoo Hoo).* When my aunt Pearl moved into a retirement home, she also gave me two sets (both from Hoo—her thing was dishes!). Storage has become a problem. I stack and store carefully, because I love to entertain, and use these treasured dishes regularly.

You'll need to make similar choices regarding dishes stored in your cupboards and china closet. Is there a set you could give away, or are there pieces that you can part with to make it easier to get to the set you use most? You can double the space of high shelves by adding another shelf (look for add-a-shelf organizers). If you don't want to have to wash dishes before using them, store them in quilted or plastic dish caddies.

As for dirty dishes, wash them and put them away!

Kitchens should be pleasant workplaces where tasks at hand can be performed in a quick, easy manner in a pleasant environment. Kitchens are not storage areas for magazines, mail, keys, personal belongings, and other clutter. They need to be decluttered so you can focus on the task at hand.

9. Reward yourself. Every time you complete a room, reward yourself in some way. Add a decorator touch to the room, go out to lunch with a friend, or buy yourself something you've been dying to have.

Principles of Organization

Now that each room has been given THE TEST and you have decluttered and simplified, more organizational skills come into play as you put things back into closets, cupboards, and drawers. The following tips will help:

1. Group like things together. In the bathroom, hair-care products can be grouped together. Prescription medications and first-aid products go together in one spot. The same goes for gift-wrap supplies—scissors, tape, ribbon, gift wrap, gift bags, greeting cards. A little girl's hair ribbons, socks, candles, and paper plates . . . Think what items are used together and group accordingly.

2. Purchase or make organizers. Bins, boxes, jars, hooks, dividers, baskets, small plastic baskets, plastic trays with labels, and files separate things from each other. Without separators the tendency is to pile everything on top of each other, creating "mess."

Dejunking is the cheapest, fastest, and most effective way to become physically and financially sound, emotionally and intellectually happy.

Don Aslett

Before purchasing, ask around, look around, and research organizing systems in hardware and variety stores. Some stores specialize in organizing systems for kitchens and closets. In most cases, see-through organizing containers are preferable so you can see at a glance what's in them. If you're looking down into an organizer, as you might do in a drawer, it hardly matters. Shoe boxes make good containers for drawers, since transparency is not necessary there. If you wish, you can add a decorator touch by covering the box with attractive contact paper that coordinates with your room.

3. Limit the number of items in each storage area. Once an area gets crowded, order is lost and mess begins. Anything being stored in current storage that's used less than once a month should be moved to a low-use area with the thought of discarding in mind. Remember, the less you have, the less you must care for. Simplify!

4. Line up items and stack with care. Once you sort through a drawer, cupboard, or shelf and get it decluttered and organized, keep the area neat and stacked. Keep linens stacked neatly on the shelf. Take pride in the order you see when you open the door.

Before you can organize, you must simplify by decluttering, getting everything that is not important out of your life. I'm not saying you should become a neurotic neatnik, but order is easier to maintain, and with less effort, when you declutter first. Clothing, silver from the silverware drawer, an extra lawn mower from the garage, music left behind from children's music lessons (the kids are now 37 and 39), magazines, or unused linens—declutter it all. Then organize it into a workable system.

Drawers

Because drawers are constantly being opened and closed and their contents shifted around, they need to be especially well organized.

- Purchase drawer dividers and customize your drawers according to your needs.
- Group like things together by color.
- Store the most frequently used items near the front of the drawer.
- Organize drawers from top to bottom, in the same order that you dress: lingerie and hose would be in upper drawers, shirts and sweaters in lower drawers.

Belts: Hang in a closet or roll to store in a drawer. (After rolling, hold belt in place with a rubber band.)

Scarves: Fold and store in a basket.

Socks: Fold in half. (Don't roll into a ball. This causes stretching and weakens the elastic.) Sock dividers can be purchased, or you can store socks in baskets.

Hose: Wash by hand or in a lingerie bag in the washing machine. To minimize snags, store each pair in a small plastic bag, one pair per bag. Sort hose by color with dividers. Label the dividers (black and navy can be difficult to discern in dim light).

Lingerie: Roll or fold bras and underpants and stack. It also works well to roll slips and camisoles. Men's underwear should be folded and stacked.

Jewelry: Pins and jewelry of all kinds should be stored in compartmentalized organizers.

Linen Closets

- Line linen closets with easy-to-clean contact paper, unless the shelves have a good painted surface.
- Fold towels in a uniform manner and stack by size and color, folds facing you.
- Fold sheets by sets. Fold sheets separately, then place the fitted sheet and pillowcases inside the flat sheet so this can be pulled out as a unit. For a neat appearance, stack sets with the fold facing you.

When storing sheets, towels, or tablecloths, place on the shelf with the fold facing you so you can remove only what you want. (If edges face out, it is difficult to determine what you have.) Tablecloths can also be hung in a closet on a pants hanger that's designed to hold multiple pairs of pants.

Simplifying and Organizing Children's Rooms

If children are going to learn the principles of simple living, their rooms must exemplify it. How can a child learn to simplify if he or she is surrounded by hundreds of toys stacked on shelves, thrown in toy boxes, packed in drawers, and crammed in closets? A child's room can, and should, be simplified, the same as other rooms.

Beds. One bed (or bunk beds) makes a good start in a child's room. The make-your-bed command can be carried out easier if a child has only a bottom sheet, a top sheet, and a comforter to worry about. One doll or stuffed animal may be placed on a bed, but don't encourage collecting a whole menagerie.

Dressers. If there is sufficient closet space, dressers can be eliminated entirely. Small children can't open drawers or see inside to retrieve or store clothing. Dressers cost money, take up valuable play space, and make cleaning more difficult. If the closet contains shelving, purchase stacking plastic baskets—one basket for socks, another for underpants, another for pajamas—again, grouping like things together.

Lower the rods for hanging clothes so children can reach and hang up their clothing without assistance. My daughter has simplified the living of her four boys by making each boy responsible for washing his laundry once a week. As he takes his clothes from the dryer, pants and shirt that form an outfit are placed on the same hanger and hung in the closet, making it easier for both mom and child.

Toys. Toy boxes should be banned! Toy boxes teach children to dump, throw, and cram. There is no organization to a toy box, and proper care for toys isn't learned by throwing them there. Simplify your child's room by having only a few toys out, ones your child is currently most interested in. Other toys can be stored neatly on top shelves in the child's closet, the family room, or the basement, and rotated. Toys can best be stored in stacking plastic bins (they take up less space), one each for Matchbox cars, Lincoln Logs, crayons, and Tinker Toys. Color books get stacked together, standing up as other books do. A child can easily select which basket he or she wishes to play with. This teaches *order*. If you live in a two-story house and the children's rooms are upstairs, keep a clutter basket at the bottom of the stairs, into which miscellaneous items are placed throughout the day. When someone goes upstairs, the basket can be taken and things put away. Keep one bin of toys in the family room that your children enjoy playing with. This might include Legos or Brio trains.

Coding kids. Another simplifying tactic that eliminates trouble among the troops is to color code hangers, toothbrushes, toy baskets, and towels.

School papers and projects. Store in a box important mementos from your child. At the end of the school year have your child select three to five favorite things to save for posterity that will go into a "treasure box" with that child's name on it. If you save 10 things per child per year for 10 years, think of the number of things you'll have to store! Do you have enough space, time, and energy to store it? Simplify, simplify!

Each child needs a place to put books, papers, and belongings upon arriving home from school. A basket or wicker tray near the door serves this purpose well. A hook by the door for backpacks is also a good idea.

Back Doors

If your family enters and leaves the house most frequently through a garage entrance or a back door, hooks or a coatrack works well for hanging jackets and backpacks. Baskets or bins placed nearby accommodate gloves and headwear.

Paper Clutter

Some of us are weighted down under piles of paper clutter that accumulate daily. And the more people who live under one roof, the more paper accumulates. Here are a few broad principles that may help you control paper clutter:

Mail. Some of our junk mail never even gets into the house—it's tossed in the garbage can on the way in. As I open letters, I check to see if I have the return address. If so, the envelope is immediately discarded. I paperclip return envelopes to bills. Harry sees only the important papers, culled from the stack and placed on his dresser. When he's through looking at them, he returns them to my office. I file bills in a file folder labeled "Bills to Pay." Letters are filed under "Letters to Answer." Magazines are stacked in one place, to be read and sorted later. Catalogues I want to keep are stacked in another area. Every time I receive an updated catalogue, I toss the old one.

Newspapers. Newspapers are an important method of communication, but as soon as a newspaper is read, it becomes obsolete and is a clutter problem. Once you fall behind in reading newspapers, you never catch up. And, like death and taxes, you can't stop them— another always appears on the morrow.

The best method of handling newspapers is daily storage and weekly disposal. Newspapers laid aside to read another time never get read. Don't try to catch up. Most of what you'd read in the paper will be recapped on television or the radio. Designate a spot in the garage or basement for old newspapers, and stack them daily. Throw them out weekly with the trash unless they're being saved for a paper drive or a recycle program.

> *The more cluttered a room, . . . the less the eye can appreciate a single item. . . . Excessive decoration, especially collections, don't just occupy physical space, but represent an investment in time and energy caring for them that could be used in relationships with people.*
>
> ELIZABETH LOWE

Magazines. Some people have stacks of magazines on coffee tables, in baskets, on the floor, overflowing magazine racks, or in boxes. Many of these people never have time to look through them but consider their magazines too precious to throw out.

Magazines are a major clutter problem. Two thirds of every magazine is clutter; 70 percent is advertising. Clip and save articles you want to read or keep as you go through the magazine the first time. File them under "Personal" for reading during personal time. Toss the remainder of the magazine.

I simply do not have time to read magazines when at home. I carry a half dozen or so onto the plane each time I board. This way, I'm able to keep up with professional journals and women's magazines I read for pleasure.

Once, on a short flight into San Francisco, I began scanning and ripping out articles immediately after boarding the plane so I could leave two or three of these magazines behind. (Magazines are heavy!) A woman seated next to me acted as if she had been personally insulted. "What are you doing to that magazine?" she asked. I told her this was my method of handling magazine clutter while I was traveling.

"Boy, do I ever need you!" she laughed. She told me an aunt had died and willed everything to her, and now her house was crammed. She also had a major magazine problem. Unsightly boxes of magazines were overrunning her home, and her cleaning lady was complaining. "I subscribe to 17 monthly magazines," she continued.

> *We make a living by what we get, but we make a life by what we give.*
>
> WINSTON CHURCHILL

I shared with her the value of sorting the clutter and getting organized. She asked to be notified the next time I was giving a seminar.

I told her story at my next home organization seminar. Suddenly a hand shot up. "Nancy," a voice called out. "Do you remember me? It's me—the woman who used to subscribe to 17 magazines. I'm down to one now and living in peace." She went on to tell how her chance meeting with me on the plane began to change her cluttered life. During the seminar she began to master other secrets to sanity and finish the job of getting her life together.

A Home Filing System

Every home needs a simple filing system. The system you select may be relegated to a drawer, portable box, or metal filing cabinet. Whatever the size and place, get something going.

For most households, five categories, with subdivisions under each major division as needed, will handle it. An attractive color-coded system works as follows:

First category: PERSONAL INTEREST (pink folders). This might include files for household ideas, decorating tips, articles to read, notes on seminars attended, minutes from organizations to which you belong, and letters to answer.

Second category: HOUSEHOLD INFORMATION (yellow folders). Here's where you file guarantees, receipts, contracts, and appliance instructions. (Unless you have a system for retrieving the instruction booklet that came with your new self-cleaning oven, you won't be able to operate the self-clean cycle safely.)

Third category: FAMILY (red folders). Each family member should have his or her own personal file folder—each in a designated color, if desired. File away school papers, notes from teachers, report cards, school pictures, and homework assignments for children. Declutter the file at the end of each school year. Papers you want to save can be stored in the child's memory box.

Fourth category: CHURCH (green folders). Church bulletins, announcements, newsletters, church directory, church business, and other related items go in this folder.

Fifth category: BILLS AND COUPONS (blue folders). As bills come in, they are immediately filed under "Bills to Pay." If you pay bills on the first and fifteenth of each month, designate one folder for each. Coupons can be collected in an envelope in another folder, where they will be easy to grab as you leave for shopping.

Storage of Items Not Currently in Use

Now gather the piles of things that need to be stored for future use (fabric scraps from sewing projects, winter clothing, craft projects, Christmas decorations, special editions of magazines, seasonal decorations)—things not currently in use, but that you plan to use someday. Here is the lowdown on storing:

Purchase boxes of uniform size and color. Forget the motley collection of banana, apple, and copy paper boxes you're currently using. Purchase matching boxes from a discount store.

Number each box. Only a number is written on the outside of the box. If you write the contents on the outside of the box, then change the contents, you'll have to scratch out. This looks messy.

Fill the box with like items to be stored.

List box contents on a file card. For example, my Christmas boxes number 1 through 12. In box 1 I find the red apple arrangement in a basket; box 2, red ornaments, garlands, and pine branches for a table arrangement; box 3, the velvet Santa, Christmas bear, Christmas towels, and tablecloths. This system saves much hassle. When I was chairperson for a quilt show and needed a specific Christmas wreath, I checked my card file and immediately located the box.

Store boxes. Boxes can be stored in the garage, basement, on upper closet shelves, or under beds. Even though you may have many boxes of stored items, there will be a sense of order because they are uniform in size and color. Now all items not currently in use are neatly stored where you can retrieve them in minutes.

Laundry

- Supplies. On a shelf near the washer keep the following supplies:
     Laundry detergent
     Prewash product
     Cleaning fluid
     Bleach
     Fabric softener
     Bar of soap
     Reference book for removal of stains
- Schedule. If just one or two of you live in the house, doing laundry one day a week works beautifully. But when you have two or more children, everything changes. You may find it easier to do several loads a day. If you get one load started before breakfast, it can be transferred to the dryer before beginning your day. Folding one load takes only a few minutes. Now that my grandsons are older, each boy has a designated hamper and wash day and is responsible for washing and drying his own clothing and hanging, folding, and putting it away. Before setting up such a plan, children must be taught how to separate clothing, operate the washer and dryer, and add detergent.
- Laundry hampers.
     Place a laundry hamper in each bedroom or bathroom.
     Teach family members to turn clothing right side out and check pockets for treasures.
     Have regular routines for wash day and have family members carry their dirty clothing to the laundry center. If there is a set day and time, there can be no excuses for not having clothing, sheets, and towels in the proper place.
- Sock management.
     Pin socks together with safety pins before washing.
     Socks can be put into a mesh bag for easier management.
     If you have more than one child who wears the same kind of socks, purchase the one-size-fits-all kind. Store them in a bin in the laundry room, and let children help themselves

as necessary.
- Putting away.
    To avoid unnecessary ironing, fold or hang items immediately as they come out of the dryer.

    Place folded clothing in appropriate baskets for distribution to the bedroom.

    Older children can pick up their own baskets and put clothing away. Laundry baskets should be returned to the laundry center.

Closet Organization

Simplicity is a principle that needs to be extended to the closet. Have in your closet only pieces of clothing you use, enjoy wearing, and feel good in. Most people spend half their time wearing clothing they are not sure meet these criteria. Simplicity also means that the less you have, the less you have to take care of. Having a few good-quality, well-designed pieces of clothing that will take you everywhere is more important than having many items of lesser quality purchased on impulse.

If we had our druthers, we'd be able to open our closet doors and find the perfect wardrobe for each occasion. Each piece would flatter our figures and coloring and suit our lifestyle. Nothing would be outdated or unnecessary. In spite of our druthers, however, most of us have bulging closets. Yet we moan, "I don't have anything to wear!" We sincerely try to dress for success and still end up with a closet full of clutter. This will continue until our closets are decluttered and everything unnecessary has been pitched. Frequently closets, drawers, and cupboards are ignored when cleaning takes place. After all, you rationalize, nobody sees in there.

According to Alexandra Stoddard, 40 percent of the contents of one's closet falls into the unnecessary category and needs to be eliminated, and 20 percent needs some form of repair or alteration. This leaves only 40 percent of what currently takes up space in your closet suitable for wear today. And it's estimated that we wear only about 20 percent of what we have packed in there. Yet we must sort through 100 percent every time we dress. We shove aside, pull out, ponder, wonder, and worry about each choice, wasting valuable time. Excess clothing adds stress to our lives. Like other clutter, we feel obligated to use it once it hangs there, whether we like it or not. Having so many choices creates a dilemma. We worry that another choice might be more appropriate, rather than enjoying the choice we've made.

When the clothing you have will not fit into a normal closet, you have too much. No closet is too small! When your closet bulges at the seams and you beg for a new house with closets the size of bedrooms, you are fooling yourself. Before you move, declutter your closet.

How to Declutter a Closet

Step 1: Begin sorting. There are two methods for decluttering a closet. One way is to remove everything from the closet (yes, everything) and begin with an empty closet. This is the method to use if you are going to add shelving or redesign the area. Clear the space and give the closet a thorough cleaning. If the closet needs a new look, now is the time to paint, wallpaper, or carpet. Paint should be high gloss so it's easy to wipe clean.

The second method is to begin sorting from a full closet, one piece at a time. This is a better method to use if all that is needed is reorganization.

Step 2: Try on every piece of clothing. Unless you have worn a piece of clothing within the past month, try it on in front of a mirror and decide its future.

Step 3: Sort clothing into five stacks.

> *Stack 1: Love-and-wear.* These articles are the right color, style, and size. They make you look and feel like a million dollars. You love and wear these pieces. Definitely keepers.
>
> *Stack 2: Clothing that needs to be washed or dry-cleaned.* Look for spots and stains.
>
> *Stack 3: Clothing that needs to be repaired or altered before it can be worn.* Check for fit, sagging hems, rips, or missing buttons.
>
> *Stack 4: Discard.* Clothing you can part with. Get rid of it if it is no longer flattering; the color, cut, or style is wrong for you; it is uncomfortable, itchy, or doesn't fit (you can't bend over or move your arms); you hardly ever (or never) wear it.
>
> *Stack 5: Ambivalent clothing.* It's important to separate *love-and-wear* clothing from *ambivalent* clothes. These pieces may be a good color but not a good fit, or a good fit but bad color, or clothes bought on sale or impulse. In other words, you're not sure if you want to keep them. Ambivalent clothing is stored in the

back of the closet (or in another closet). It is a holding tank, of sorts, until you make up your mind about its final destination.

Put dirty clothing into the clothes hamper. Clothing that needs to go to the cleaners should be put into a bag ready to go to the car. Clothing that needs repair goes to another area. Make immediate plans either to repair it yourself or have it done—or dump it.

I go through my wardrobe thoroughly twice a year—March (as the California season leaves winter behind) and October (as we leave warm weather behind). I put what no longer fits into a discard pile that is destined for a consignment store that sells clothing for me and sends me a check when items sell. Then I have the fun of going on a guilt-free shopping spree. I beg you not to become like the woman I heard about who keeps clothing in five sizes so she has something to wear regardless of her current weight.

As I bring winter clothing into our walk-in closet, I check each piece. If it seems outdated, soiled, in poor repair, or if I'm just plain tired of it, that item never gets hung up. This helps me weed out nonessentials and allows me to purchase new clothing.

Blessed is the home where God is at home and where the spirit of Christ rules.
THEODORE F. ADAMS

Step 4: Replace all wire hangers. Wire hangers bend easily and allow clothing to smash together. They are unattractive and cause horizontal creases across the knees of pants. Invest in tubular plastic hangers. In addition to being sturdy, they keep clothing evenly spaced, preventing wrinkling. They are great for rust-free drip drying and can be purchased in decorator colors. If you like, the color of the hanger can denote the category—blue for dressy outfits, yellow for sports clothing, green for work clothing, etc.

The average woman needs about 100 hangers. Men need fewer, because business suits and sports jackets should be hung on curved wooden hangers. Treasure every padded hanger you own. Hang dressy jackets and dresses on these or the clear plastic hangers that come with the purchase of a new dress.

Step 5: Put the clothing you love and wear back into the closet. Be sure that it's clean and fits, is becoming in color, and is in good repair. Once you get this far, you'll likely find that your once-crowded closet looks roomier.

Hang clothing facing you (if yours is a walk-in closet) or facing in the same direction. Button top buttons.

Group like things together. Categories for my lifestyle are as follows: dressy suits and jackets, dressy blouses, cotton blouses, and knit tops. On the lower rod I have several jogging suits, casual outfits, and pants, hung together by color, with dresses hung at the back. Even small closets can be rebuilt and redesigned to provide more usable space. If you have a second closet in another room, you can store clothing not currently in season until needed again.

Step 6: Get shoes off the floor. Remove all shoes from the closet. Shoes that lie on the floor get kicked around and become a jumbled, dusty mess. The best place for shoes is lined up on a shelf in plastic see-through boxes. These could be placed on a shelf above the clothes rack, or in a wall unit installed for shoe storage. When we had our closet redesigned, we had shoe slots installed against the wall. A third-best system is a shoe bag or shoe rack that hangs from the closet door. Whatever the location, you must be able to vacuum the closet floor with ease. Select only shoes that are in good repair and are the right color and size to go back into your much-improved closet. Dump the rest.

Step 7: Sort through handbags. Remove all handbags stored in the closet, making decisions about each one. Discard old, misshapen, or rarely used bags. For ease in selection, store the rest in clear plastic bags on an upper shelf.

Step 8: Hats. Hats can be stored in hatboxes, on shelves, or hung on the wall if you have room.

Step 9: All other items. Take out every other item in your closet and make a decision about what to do with it: put away, give away, or sell. The vacuum cleaner, picture albums, linens, and tennis racquets do not belong in your clothes closet.

Closet Decor. If you want to enjoy your newly organized closet, it must delight your eye when you open the door. Closet space can be decorated with paint, wallpaper, or posters. If you use wallpaper, stick with miniprints or subtle patterns so the decor doesn't overpower the size of the room, or the color or fabric of your clothing. Another idea is to make a collage of some of the pretty cards you've received from special people in your life and tape them to the walls. That way, you can enjoy the memory of their friendship every day.

If your closet is not well lit, install proper lighting so you can see your choices at a glance, rather than groping in the dark. A small step stool for an easy reach to upper shelves is helpful. Should you be fortunate enough to have a room-sized closet, hang a full-length or three-way mirror for checking your appearance after dressing. A bench or chair that offers seating while you're putting on shoes and socks is another plus.

Your closet has the potential for making you look and feel your best. Set it up in such a way that you can best express the way you want to look and feel.

Now you can relax. Closets don't need to be cleaned as often as the rest of the house. And closets are not open for public viewing, usually not even for the rest of the family. Yes, this area of your home needs organization, but you can view it with a more relaxed attitude. As long as it stays neat and gets periodic maintenance, it's useless effort to make your closet a showplace and to spend endless time, money, and effort on this area of your home.

Now that your closet is cleaned, how about a look into those drawers!

Underclothing. Chances are your closet looks better than your lingerie drawers. Most of us at least group blouses together in a closet, but our underwear drawers often resemble a white sale table at Macy's. Underwear should be grouped in drawer organizers. I use small plastic baskets to separate bras from panties and slips. Hosiery can be grouped together in dividers. Look for dividers that suit your needs and get things in shape.

> *Make it a point to do something every day that you don't want to do. This is the golden rule for acquiring the habit of doing your duty without pain.*
> MARK TWAIN

When organizing lingerie, take everything out of the drawer, wipe the drawer clean, and line it with new drawer paper. Then put back only what is in good repair, fits well, and is attractive. Underwear is the most intimate of our clothing items and should be attractive. Discard all lingerie that does not enhance your appearance; this will affect the way you feel about yourself. You do not want to be uncomfortable all day long because you are tugging or pulling at something that is ill-fitting. Throw out everything that doesn't make you look and feel pretty—and I don't care what size you are. It is better to have a few pretty items that fit than hordes of ugly old ones.

Jewelry, scarves, and other accessories. The drawer designated to hold these items should bring delight when you open it, and not display a jumbled mess of belts tangled in scarves. Belts can be hung in the closet or neatly rolled and stacked in a small basket or divider. Pins and other jewelry should be laid out neatly for easy viewing and accessibility in a jewelry box or organizer. Fold scarves and store inside a small plastic basket. As with clothing, sort and return to your drawer only accessories that fit, that are the right color, and that you love and use.

Orderly drawers can become a rainbow of color and bring delight to your eyes when you open them if you take a few minutes to make them look this way. Once you get your drawers organized, you can easily maintain order on a daily basis. If belts are tossed back into the drawer without being rolled again, within a week all that you've accomplished will be destroyed.

Pajamas, nightgowns, bathrobes, and peignoirs. If I could peek into the drawer where your nightgowns are housed, what would I find? That oldie with grease spots down the front? Yes, the lace is torn and the gathers are pulled out at the waist, and you are still wearing it! Get rid of the old, faded, and torn nightclothes that clutter this area. The clothes we sleep in should be soft and lovely. We can hardly feel feminine in a torn, faded, spotted nightgown. Get yourself a new nightie!

Clothes make strong impressions on our emotions. The memories connected with each outfit greatly affect our moods and behaviors. If you associate something with pleasant memories, you will likely have a delightful day. If you receive raves from coworkers when you wear yellow, this evokes pleasant memories. Eliminate those articles that depress you.

Take care of your clothing. Remember, when you dress for the day, you are preparing yourself for an adventure. How your clothing is housed makes an enormous difference in the way you think about yourself and how you will act and feel during the day.

Here's a rule to help you stay within limits: every time you purchase a new item, an old one must go. This goes for every item of clothing in your closet or drawers. If you bring home a new pair of shoes, an old pair must go. By continually and carefully editing your wardrobe, you can maintain a clutter-free closet. If you don't, eventually you must go back and redo the massive closet decluttering. Avoid falling into the same trap again!

Life Without Clutter

How long you want to deal with the issue of clutter is up to you. But it will hold you back from becoming the person you can and should be. Clutter has a price tag, both to acquire and to maintain it. If you really want to live the life you should be living, the things that clutter your home and life need to be disposed of *now*. Once you experience the freedom of clutter-free living, it is almost like being "born again"!

Everything that clutters your home will also clutter your mind, depriving you of time and energy that could be directed toward more important things. Once we get rid of the clutter, we gain a sense of freedom and clarity of thinking.

Life doesn't really begin at 40. Life begins when you declutter your home and establish a more carefree lifestyle. Getting a junk-free home raises your standard of living, gives you back time and energy that all this "stuff" stole from you. You'll be more physically and emotionally healthy. There will be more harmony in your home, more time for loving and being loved, more time for sharing, serving, being satisfied, inspired, and joyful.

---

*If you don't know who Hoo Hoo is, you'll have to read chapter 1 of my book *Creative Hospitality*.

Belle Star's Closet: A four-pole design for a woman who likes things just so. Every inch of space is used wisely.

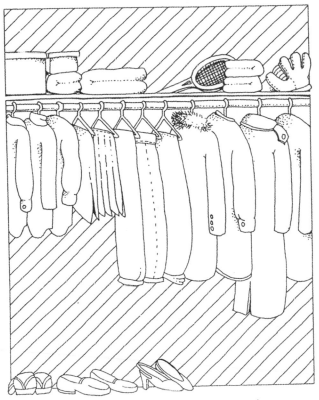

The areas marked with parallel lines show you how much space is wasted in the average closet. There are so many ways to use this space as you'll see on the following pages.

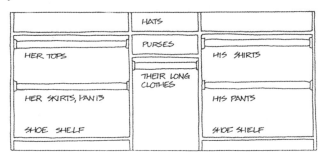

	HATS	
HER TOPS	PURSES	HIS SHIRTS
	THEIR LONG CLOTHES	
HER SKIRTS, PANTS		HIS PANTS
SHOE SHELF		SHOE SHELF

The Jack Sprat's Closet: A simple design for a closet for two. Five poles are used with four shelves.

Sort Through the Clutter

Assignments:

Give each room in your home THE TEST. Reward yourself for a job well done as each room is completed.

CLUTTER CONTROL:

For personal devotions read Ecclesiastes 3:1-6:
> "There is a time for everything,
>> and a season for every activity under the heaven:
>>> a time to be born and a time to die,
>>> a time to plant and a time to uproot,
>>> a time to kill and a time to heal,
>>> a time to tear down and a time to build,
>>> a time to weep and a time to laugh,
>>> a time to mourn and a time to dance,
>>> a time to scatter stones and a time to gather them,
>>> a time to embrace and a time to refrain,
>>> a time to search and a time to give up,
>>> a time to keep and a time to throw away" (NIV).

These verses say to me: _____

_____

_____

As a result of what these verses tell me, I will _____

_____

_____

*The biggest obstacle in getting
your life in order is yourself!*

AFFIRMATION
for Secret to Sanity 5

*T*oday I choose to put order in my life.
I can and will begin to sort through the
multiplicity of things that clutter my home
and closets. I realize this may take time. I will keep
a positive frame of mind throughout the process and
reward myself as each room is completed.
It can be done, and it can be fun!

Lift your spirits—go the extra mile

1. Take a fresh look at your front hall table. If it has become cluttered, straighten it, toss the clutter, and rearrange all the objects. Now look at the table through fresh eyes. Perhaps it's time for a pick-me-up. Free yourself to let go of the old and tired to make way for the new and exciting.

2. When you know you have a tough day ahead of you, wear your favorite outfit or prettiest color. You will feel more confident and be better able to handle stress.

3. Add a creative touch to one of your rooms today. As your family changes, your rooms can change. Rearrange objects, move furniture, hang a new painting. Little touches can bring great satisfaction!

And one inexpensive item can prevent dirt from entering your home in the first place: a mat at every entrance.

SECRET TO SANITY 6:

HOW TO CLEAN LIKE A PRO

merica's self-appointed cleaning guru, Don Aslett, understands how to take the work out of cleaning. According to him, a home could be almost maintenance-free by digging and carpeting a sunken living room—which is exactly what he did. He padded his living room, an octagonal conversation pit, with vinyl-backed cushions, where 12 to 14 people could sit and visit comfortably. Ten or 12 more could gather on padded, two-tiered bleachers facing those in the pit. There was no furniture in the house except for beds and a dining room table and chairs. Everything else—TV, stereo components, and bookcases—was built in. The bedrooms were devoid of nightstands and dressers that collect and display clutter, and beds were mounted on pedestal bases. All clothing was hung in closets, stored on shelving, or kept in built-in drawers.

Another Aslett suggestion: Mount sofas and other furniture on hydraulics so that at the press of a button they rise automatically to allow for easy, unhindered vacuuming and dusting. His assessment of how to take the work out of housework is accurate and amusing, but not aesthetically pleasing to the eye. Our homes need to be functional, easy to clean, *and* attractive.

The How-to's of Cleaning

How do other people get their homes clean? Some don't. Others don't have children. Still others hire a cleaning service, get their husbands and children to do it all, or simply sweep the dirt under the rug. Maybe they use only one room in the house or simply bolt the door. However, most of us muddle along, relying on what we learned by watching our mothers bending over and scrubbing things with strong-smelling solutions. Your mother probably didn't give you many lessons on *how* to clean. The truth is, most of us have had precious little training in how to clean a house efficiently and effectively.

All the hints from Heloise, advice from Dear Abby, gimmicks, and formulas aren't the answer. But there are proven ways to have and maintain a clean house. It all begins with learning techniques for preventing housework and learning professional methods for cleaning. Housecleaning can become a creative task and be fun (well, maybe not as much fun as an afternoon of shopping at Nordstrom or Macy's). It's possible to create a clean home environment and an organized, easy-to-maintain home that welcomes family and friends and makes an important contribution.

A clean house can and will get messed up again, but you can't mess up the improvements to quality of life your efforts have produced. How you live in and care for your dwelling shapes your personality—and your destiny. Home is the center of civilization.

DON ASLETT

A Personal Daily Plan enables you to record things before you forget them. But the list won't do the jobs for you. A card system, recommended by some, sets schedules and regimens. However, we need to take a careful look at how we use our time and budget it accordingly. A PDP should not dictate every move; it's up to you to control your PDP for your benefit, not the reverse.

Most housecleaners have been brought up with the idea to "clean house once a week" according to predetermined spotless criteria. On this day all dust, dirt, spiders, and critters are brought up for review and extermination. Then exhaustion sets in.

One woman recalls her mother's approach to housecleaning. "Every Friday Mom would begin early in the morning," she recalls. "The house would be vacuumed and dusted, the windows washed, and furniture polished. In the afternoon she would cook. By Friday evening she would have accomplished it all. Friday evening was family worship time, when we were supposed to enjoy each other, read stories, and sing together after supper. But Mom was so exhausted after her daylong housecleaning attack that she couldn't enjoy our evening together. And we didn't want to be around her."

Such housecleaning methods get you little further than to an early grave. Even if you do end up with a clean house, the negative experience will offset the few rewards. It's not so much what product you clean with as how you go about it that really matters. If you follow the simple professional methods that follow, you'll get your home clean faster and easier.

The First Rule of Cleaning: Prevent Dirt From Getting Inside

The first rule of cleaning is to avoid it. That's right—not having to do it in the first place! Certain tasks, such as doing dishes, can't be avoided (unless you want to eat directly from the pot). But other difficult cleaning tasks can be made lighter or avoided altogether simply by following certain prevention techniques.

1. Mat every entrance to your home. According to Don Aslett, it's been calculated that the average five-person house accumulates 40 pounds of dust and dirt per year. The greatest proportion of this grit and dirt is carried into the house via clothes and shoes. Professionals estimate it costs $600 a pound to remove dirt once it's inside. Why so much?

- Carpets must be shampooed.
- Floors must be stripped and waxed.
- More dust is created because of dirt circulating in the air.
- Clothes must be washed more frequently.
- Extra dirt wears out cleaning equipment more rapidly.

And one inexpensive item can prevent dirt from entering your home in the first place: a mat at every entrance (and don't forget the garage entrances). It takes only a broom and a few minutes to get dirt out of a mat, but it takes 10 pieces of equipment and hours of work to get it out of your house!

One such mat, Mr. Brush-Step, is available at discount stores. A commercial grade of matting is also available at janitorial supply houses. The nylon exterior creates a static charge that helps pull dirt particles from clothing and shoes. The rough texture helps wipe dirt and grime from shoes.

A 3' x 5' mat will cover three to four steps and lasts as many as 15 years. It absorbs mud and water, does not easily show dirt, and can be vacuumed or swept like other carpet. It can be hosed down, scrubbed with an all-purpose cleaner, and hung up to dry.

A "matted" home is not only cleaner, but safer. The throw rugs you may be using in your doorways aren't good for much except throwing people's backs out when they slip and fall on them. Besides that, they are unattractive.

2. Eat only in designated areas. In some families it's an accepted practice to take plates of food and snacks into the family room, bedroom, or in front of the television. (Once this habit gets started, you'll have a tough time breaking it.) It's only a matter of time until a spill occurs. Food spills make big messes and are difficult, if not impossible, to clean up. If family members want to eat in front of the television for special occasions, plan for it by spreading out a plastic tablecloth and creating an indoor picnic atmosphere. Generally speaking, food should be eaten at the table or breakfast bar area—and never on upholstered furniture. Futhermore, meals together should become cherished memories. Time spent eating together should become treasured time.

3. Establish routines for washing up. Children should wash their hands not only before they come to the table, but when they leave the table. Fingers, sticky with peanut butter, jam, honey, and grease, touch walls, woodwork, and furniture. Children should also wash up when they come in from playing outside.

4. Confine crafts to a specific area. Encouraging children to engage in coloring, painting, and other craft projects is admirable. But permit this in specific areas only, and on a surface that can be easily wiped up. Never allow children to engage in craft projects on carpeting. Felt-tip markers and other arts and craft supplies can be very hard on upholstered furniture.

5. Eliminate airborne dirt. Sheer curtains hung at windows can capture airborne dust and dirt and are easily washable. They should be drawn, especially when windows are open. Air-conditioning and air purifiers are also helpful.

6. Scotchgard carpets and upholstered furniture. Scotchgard, a trade name for a soil retardant, is used on carpets, rugs, or upholstery and guards against penetration of soils and stains. It preserves and protects, making upholstery and carpets look better and wear longer.

The Second Rule of Cleaning:
Clean With Professional Concentrates

How many chemical products and cleaners currently clutter cupboards, under-sink areas, and utility closets in your home? The majority of these cleaners not only take up valuable space, present safety hazards for children, and may actually damage surfaces, but are ineffective.

There are some people who purchase every exotic new product for cleaning. Clean is good, but why store a raft of cleaning supplies and gadgets that outnumber the items needing cleaning? Chances are you don't need a fraction of the products that currently clutter your utility closet. Keeping cleaning supplies organized becomes simpler when just the basics are stocked.

1. All-purpose cleaners. Any time you purchase a concentrate you save 80 percent. I recommend Tru-Test Professional Concentrated All-purpose Cleaner CC-11, available at True Value hardware stores.* I mix it according to directions and store it in a plastic spray bottle, labeled with a waterproof marker. It leaves no residue (even in the hardest water), removes soap scum, is odor-freshened, biodegradable, does not foam, and is USDA-authorized. From this cleaner, which I purchase by the quart, I make my own all-purpose cleaner for floors, painted and most hard surfaces, and automotive exteriors. It is not recommended for glass or unsealed wood surfaces.

Our true home is inside each of us. Our houses are the outward expression of something we have already achieved.

ALEXANDRA STODDARD

The appropriate solution can be applied with a spray bottle, mop, brush, sponge, or cleaning cloth. Several minutes should be allowed for soaking time, depending on soil buildup. Residue should be removed with mop, wet-vac, power rinse, squeegee, sponge, or cleaning cloth. Then rinse with water. I have used this product for years and find it superior to anything purchased in supermarkets. It gives outstanding results on surfaces ordinary cleaners can't touch.

2. Bathroom cleaner. Bathrooms need a germicidal action and a disinfectant cleaner. True Value also makes Tru-Test Professional Concentrated Germicidal Cleaner DC-6.† This cleaner/disinfectant is recommended for hospitals, nursing homes, schools, veterinary clinics, and households. It can be used on all hard, nonporous surfaces, such as floors, walls, tabletops, metals, plastics, and porcelain. Applied with a mop, sponge, cleaning cloth, or spray bottle, it disinfects, cleans, and deodorizes in one labor-saving step, and is effective against a long list of pathogenic bacteria.

Mix your own solution by the quart and store it in a spray bottle. You'll find cleaning bathrooms will become easier and more pleasant, and your household will be more sanitary and healthier.

3. *Mirrors and windows.* Another spray bottle is needed for this cleaner, which I mix up myself (the dishwashing soap helps the cleaning tool glide over the glass surface, and the ammonia cuts the film):

> 1 quart water
> 2 to 3 drops liquid dishwashing detergent
> 1 tablespoon ammonia

Almost all my cleaning is done with the all-purpose cleaner, the disinfectant cleaner, and my own formula for mirrors and windows. An all-purpose cleaner can handle most household cleaning jobs, but if you have a specialized job, match your cleaning agent to the job you're doing. If you don't know what to use, call or visit a janitorial supply store and ask.

That we are alive today is proof positive that God has something for us to do today.

LINDSAY

There's no magic formula for cleaning, but very few supplies are needed. The rule of simplicity is the most effective. When you use the right product, the job can be done faster and better. You'll spend a lot less money on cleaning supplies if you select them carefully and use them properly. You'll also protect surfaces from deteriorating.

By organizing your cleaning supplies and the way you clean, you'll gain more time for yourself. And once you've cleared out the clutter, you'll find that it becomes significantly easier to maintain clutter-free space on a regular basis.

The Third Rule of Cleaning: Give the Cleaner Time to Clean

We work too hard when cleaning; we scrub and scrub. For years we've used this method on sinks, countertops, shower stalls, floors, and multiple other places. But if the area were first thoroughly sprayed or dampened with an all-purpose cleaner and allowed to soak, it could be wiped up with greater ease. The way to remove dirt and soil is not by scraping, grinding, and scrubbing, but by applying the right solution and waiting. It's time to use our brains instead of elbow grease when it comes to cleaning dirty surfaces.

There are four steps to cleaning:

Step 1: Surface-clean. Sweep, dust-mop, brush, or wipe all loose surface dirt and particles from the area to be cleaned.

Step 2: Saturate area with cleaning solution. Spray or apply cleaning solution generously to the area to be cleaned.

Step 3: Wait one to three minutes. Let the all-purpose cleaner—not you—do the work If you immediately begin scrubbing, you aren't allowing the chemicals to do their job.

Step 4: Remove residue. With a cleaning cloth, sponge, or squeegee, wipe up the mucky residue. It takes only minutes to complete the total job—with much less work.

The Fourth Rule of Cleaning: Clean With Proper Tools

Where do you purchase quality cleaning equipment? The supermarket and discount store are not the right places. Professional equipment is better than household equipment. Both good-quality hardware stores and janitorial supply houses are the places to go. Proper cleaning tools may be a little more expensive, but one well-made tool will last a long time and give better results.

Here's a list of tools that should be in every home to make cleaning easier.

CLEANING TOOLS AND SUPPLIES

CLEANING TOOLS	TOTE SUPPLIES
Broom	Cleaning cloths
Dustpan	All-purpose cleaner
Dry mop	Bathroom cleaner
Sponge mop	Window cleaner
Bucket	Treated dustcloth
Window squeegee	Old knife
Whisk broom	Toothbrush
Furniture brush	Clean paintbrush
Lamb's wool duster	Toilet bowl screen
Toilet brush	Rubber gloves
Upright vacuum cleaner	Knee pads
Hand floor scrubber	Cellulose sponge
	Scrubbing sponge
	Nylon-bristled scrub brush

Keep your cleaning tools within reach. Someone has estimated that a homemaker walks eight to 15 miles a day while doing housework. Walking is good for us, but I'd rather do it in the sunshine than inside my house while rushing here and there searching for tools. Certain cleaning supplies must be kept at a central "cleaning station." But all-purpose spray should be kept where it is used most frequently. A spray bottle of your bathroom cleaner should be kept in each bathroom, along with a spray bottle for mirrors. This will save endless time in running to the other end of the house, or even trotting downstairs to the cleaning station for a tote.

Cleaning cloths. One of the big reasons professional house cleaners can clean a home so quickly is that they use professional equipment. The most famous cleaning tool of all is known as "the rag." If I were to check out the area where you stash rags, what would I find? Torn sheets? Tattered diapers? Shirt and pajama remnants? Holey T-shirts? Slips? For the past several decades fabric manufacturers have attempted to produce fabrics that repel liquids and stains. Homemakers dip these fabrics into solvents and solutions and try to clean with them. The truth is, rags are ineffective cleaning tools. They can't clean effectively because they aren't designed to do the job they are used for.

The best cleaning cloths are made from a poly/cotton fabric blend. The cotton content gives the fabric its pile (nap), and the polyester helps the fabric to dry faster and resist wrinkles. When I switched from rags to cleaning cloths, I didn't have to go far. I had seen stacks of towels on a shelf in the garage. Harry orders everything by the dozen or in lots of 100. He had ordered these towels from a janitor supply store to use in wiping his hands after working on the car. I asked him for 20 of them and have been happily using them ever since.

You may not have 100 of them in your garage, but you can purchase what you need at the discount store of your choice. Twenty cleaning cloths are usually enough to equip any home. Cleaning cloths that are uniform in size and shape fold neatly for easy, attractive storage. Terrycloth makes an excellent cleaning cloth, and even protects your hands while you're cleaning. And don't dump all your rags in the dumpster. Save a few for paint and grease cleanup.

When you complete your cleaning task and the cloths are damp and dirty, toss them in the washer. Don't stuff them under a sink in the crook of the pipes, or any other place. Wash them immediately. Over a period of time your cloths will get dingy and stained, but they will be just as clean. Fold them in fourths and store them in a small plastic basket and you will have just decluttered another area of your home. No more piles of rags stored all over the place.

The Fifth Rule of Cleaning: Simplify Living Space
You've already decluttered your home, which automatically speeds

the cleaning process. But we need to take the concept of decluttering to the next level.

Would you rather clean a room containing four tables, six chairs, seven standing plants, two floor lamps, three magazine racks, two speakers, and matching ceramic dogs—or a room with none of the above? Take a critical look at each room. Which pieces are necessary for function in this room? Which can be eliminated? Take out what isn't necessary and obtain more open space. You'll gain living space and find the room easier to clean. In the process you are simplifying your living space and making it easier to clean.

No one wants to live in a home without furnishings. Bare floors, stark ceilings, and blank walls would hardly be aesthetically enjoyable. However, you would be able to notice everything about the room—shadows, proportions, colors, how light enters—in a way that you cannot in a room full of furniture.

Whereas few people want to live in empty rooms, the manner in which a room is furnished can simplify cleaning—or make it more difficult. Let's look at each room of your home with an eye for simplifying.

The living room. Living rooms are created for entertaining friends. Few families live in the living room. A few strong statements in this room that best represent you are all that are necessary. A well-designed L-shaped sofa makes as good use of space as do two matching sofas if you do a lot of group entertaining. Any time you have more than three sofas, a room looks overwhelmed. Occasional chairs can always be added for more seating.

> *There is a difference between striving for excellence, and striving for perfection. The first is attainable, gratifying, and healthy. The second is unattainable, frustrating, and neurotic. It is also a terrible waste of time.*
> Edwin Bliss

Coffee tables. The coffee table is the only table necessary in the living room. One floral arrangement or one art object is all that should adorn the table. Any more than three pieces on a coffee table make it cluttered, regardless of the size.

End tables. End tables simply aren't necessary except for aesthetics or lamps. You can save money (and endless dusting) by not purchasing them in the first place. Overhead lighting works wonders.

Speakers. Hang speakers. Better yet, place them in a wall unit. When they sit on the floor they collect dust *and* ornaments, not to mention that they take up floor space.

Lamps. Too many lamps give a room a choppy appearance. Floor lamps are preferable to table lamps, as they can be moved more easily when cleaning and don't need a table. Consider recessed, track, or hanging lights to eliminate the problem of too many lamps in a room.

A simple but elegantly decorated living room might contain an L-shaped sofa, a generous coffee table, track lighting or a floor lamp, a beautiful painting or two, a large plant to soften the corner of the room, a fireplace, and miniblinds to adjust light.

Plants. Plants add life and color to a room, bringing a sense of outdoors inside. But they also drop leaves, spill dirt, leak water, and create a mess. It takes time to water, fertilize, spray, repot, and talk to them. Even so, some rooms need a plant or two. You might settle for one large plant, rather than a multiplicity of small plants throughout the house.

The true calling of a Christian is not to do extraordinary things, but to do ordinary things in an extraordinary way.

DEAN STANLEY

Idea: If a room needs the "life" of a green plant, buy a silk ficus (so easy to care for!). If a room needs color, buy a pot of blooming flowers. Keep them for a month, then plant them outside or throw them away.

Bedrooms. Master bedrooms are designed primarily for sleeping, dressing, and relaxing. The presence of a desk, paperwork, TV, VCR, and things to do complicates a bedroom and makes it appear stressful and cluttered.

Beds. A mattress placed on a platform or drawer base is the simplest and easiest bed to maintain. It eliminates under-the-bed space that collects dust and clutter. Platform beds with drawers for storing linens eliminate the trek down the hallway for sheets and pillowcases.

Comforters. Instead of blankets and a bedspread, choose a beautiful decorator comforter. Bedmaking becomes a breeze.

Pillows. Ten decorator pillows piled high on a bed look beautiful and inviting. But it takes time to set them aside before crawling into your bed at night, and more time to put them back in the morning. It takes time to select them, money to buy them, and time to repair them. Prune down the number of pillows, dolls, and other cutesy items on your bed.

Dressers. Whenever possible, eliminate dressers. Dresser tops collect clutter. Drawers take time to open and shut. Time is spent organizing personal belongings to keep them in order.

So where can you keep your "stuff"? Walk-in closets with organized shelving are best. Some of us may not currently have that option, but keep it in mind when purchasing a new home or remodeling. It may be worth the price to upgrade to a home with walk-in closet space so you can enjoy empty, uncluttered space in your bedroom. Small bedrooms feel more spacious without dressers. (A silk ficus might look gorgeous where the dresser used to be.)

Nightstands. Like dressers, nightstands can be major clutter collectors. If you wish to keep them, declutter the top, allowing only one or two things on the surface. Dusting instantly becomes easier.

Windows. A simplified bedroom features miniblinds, not fluffy curtains or heavy draperies that collect dust and must be dry-cleaned. Miniblinds regulate light and have a sleek appearance. Weekly maintenance will keep them from becoming major cleaning problems. For easier dusting, keep windowsills clear of clutter.

Bathrooms. The bathroom probably sees you at your worst. But this room also offers comfort—warm showers or baths to help you get ready to meet your day. Bathrooms should be kept simple so you can get ready quickly, and offer comfort when you need a few minutes alone to attend to body functions.

Shower doors: Keep a cloth handy for wiping down the shower door after each use. A squeegee works well for large glass showers. Excellent prevention for mildew and cleaning problems. And prevention is the key!

Kitchens. Counter areas should look sleek and orderly. Every item placed on the kitchen counter must be moved for cleaning and gets in the way of meal preparation and cooking (toaster, blender, mixer, or crock of wooden spoons). Frequency of use and space available will dictate what should be left out on the counter.

Empty space. Empty, uncluttered space can be peaceful to live with, look at, and enjoy. Cleared flat surfaces and fewer pieces of furniture create order and simple beauty that frees your mind to think creatively. Having fewer things helps us enjoy what we do have.

"Careless" fabrics, colors, and patterns. There are many fabrics, finishes, and colors that clean so easily that maintenance is a minor task. The more of these you include in your home, the less work you will have. As you make decorating decisions, bear in mind that floors, carpets, and fabrics can be badly damaged if not maintained regularly. Those who do not wish to care regularly for finishes should choose soil-resistant finishes. It's no secret that homes with young children are more difficult to maintain. Cleaning and picking up after them is work enough without compounding your efforts by having fragile, hard-to-clean surfaces and furnishings.

Patterns, prints, and colors. Rooms are often filled with too many patterns, prints, and colors. If one wishes to display fine pieces of furniture or art treasures, open space and plain backgrounds are needed. Check each room to see if you have more patterns or colors than necessary.

Although whites, pastels, and light colors make space appear larger, they also show more soil. Be discreet in the use of dark colors as well. It's true that soil and stains won't show up so much on chocolate-brown carpets or a navy couch, but dust and lint will.

Medium tones blend in with dirt and are a possible balance between light and dark. Muted colors, such as beige or mauve, show soil less than vibrant yellows and pinks.

> *With only plain rice to eat, with only water to drink, and with only an arm for a pillow, I am still content.*
>
> CONFUCIOUS

A patterned wallpaper with a lot of white in it can give the same feeling of size and openness without showing every fingerprint. Nubby textures create shadows and help disguise soil on fabric and carpet.

Carpets. When purchasing a new home or installing new carpet, remember that some carpet colors camouflage dirt and heavy-use paths; others highlight it. Solid color carpeting shows traffic trails worse than a patterned one. Medium earth tones are best for minimizing the appearance of dirt and wear. Extremely light or dark colors work to your disadvantage more than do colors in midtones.

Upholstery fabrics. Natural fabrics that are frequently offered in white, such as cottons and heavy canvases, are difficult to maintain. Soft cottons absorb soil and wear out quickly. Canvas retains dirt and is very difficult, if not impossible, to clean. A washable blend of natural and synthetic fibers, or all synthetic, is your best bet. Scotchgarding, or a similar treatment, helps fabric remain resistant to soil and stain. For best results, Scotchgarding should be done professionally.

Simple elegance. Uncluttered, simply decorated rooms can be esthetically pleasing and lend themselves to a style of elegance all their own. A room can become a neutral background against which you can display precious items of color and texture. Prime importance should be given to the natural patterns of sunlight that play on surfaces throughout the day.

Simple living does not mean living in stark, colorless surroundings. It means choosing what goes into a room to make it pleasing to the eye, comfortable, and yet easy to care for. A home should be designed to offer a restful retreat for family members. The less clutter and the easier the care, the more opportunity there is for every member of the family to enjoy the home.

The Sixth Rule of Cleaning:
Put the GO Principle to Work for You

The GO Principle of work management states that it is more efficient to do as much as possible of one type of work before changing to another. Management specialists have identified a warm-up period when a job is first begun, but before efficiency has been reached. Peak efficiency is dubbed GO (for Greatest Output). In other words, when any task is tackled at one time—say, the entire house is dusted or all the vacuuming is done—we work on a higher plateau of GO than the person who jumps from job to job and back again.

The GO theory shoots holes in any system that teaches you to clean one room per day. It also debunks the theory that we should try to keep the dishes washed as we cook. If you attempt to keep up with the dishes while cooking, you interrupt yourself and lose speed every few minutes in order to wash a dish here and there. Time would be better used if you finished all your cooking and then did all the dishes.

On the other hand, stay in tune with your body rhythms so you know when your GO is about spent and you should switch to another job. This means you should warm up doing a job and get going strong, but switch to another task before you decide you can't stand it one more minute. Warm up and GO with one; but switch before tiring.

Sometimes the hardest part of any job is getting started. We can all think of the most elaborate excuses or foolish reasons for not beginning a job. A Personal Daily Plan helps you warm up to a job. On your way home from work, remind yourself about what task needs to be completed and plot your method for accomplishing it. If the task is vacuuming, begin thinking it through. After supper, ask one of the children to bring the vacuum to the family room and vacuum the areas that he or she can easily do. You can finish the more difficult areas where furniture is involved. You are already warming up by thinking this through ahead of time.

The Seventh Rule of Cleaning: Rotate Thoroughness

Another principle of efficiency comes into play here. Rotate thoroughness in each task. For example, one week I vacuum the family and dining areas thoroughly, moving small pieces of furniture, chairs, standing lamps, bookcases, etc. The rest of the house gets a thorough job in the main traffic areas. The next week the living room receives a thorough going over, while the family room and the rest of the house receive vacuuming in the main traffic areas only. A simple method of rotation in this manner means that every carpeted room in your home can receive a thorough vacuuming every four to six weeks. Apply the same techniques to dusting and other tasks.

Cleaning Know-how

When informal surveys are conducted regarding women's favorite household chores, the number one favorite is vacuuming. In reality, vacuuming is preceded by hiring a cleaning service, turning on the dishwasher, and completing any task. The number two favorite? Dusting and polishing. Number three is washing clothes.

The most dreaded chore list could probably go on forever, but at the top is cleaning bathrooms. A close second is cleaning windows, followed by cleaning ovens and doing dishes.

Such information doesn't do much to edify our lives or improve our approach to housecleaning. But if there is any truth in the adage that misery loves company, you probably have some company in your likes and dislikes. Whether dreaded or favorite, let's look at individual tasks, master the basics, and do them right.

Carpets. With a little know-how carpets can look better. And the work of keeping them looking good can be minimized. If you are moving into a new home or replacing old carpet, think quality. Most carpet on the market today is good quality, but it costs only a few dollars more to upgrade to the best. Carpet is a choice you live with for many years, and if you don't choose wisely, you pay a heavy price in durability, comfort, enjoyment, and ease of maintenance.

Though carpet is easier to maintain than hardwood floors, the biggest problem with carpet is neglect. Homeowners let it go too long —and then it cannot be restored. Damage to carpet comes not from foot traffic alone, but from residues—dust, sand, grit, and dirt—that are allowed to remain on the carpet. When this debris is walked on and ground in, the carpet gets soiled and damaged on top and on the bottom. To maintain carpet properly, surface dirt needs to be removed before getting ground in.

Therefore, a good carpet cleaning system includes installing mats at every entrance to your home, then regularly vacuuming the carpets and mats. Just because you can't see dirt embedded in the carpet doesn't mean it isn't there. With good care and regular maintenance it is possible to let your carpeting go for many years before it needs shampooing. Shampooing will not harm your carpets or cause them to get dirty any faster than washing a pair of socks causes them to become dirty more quickly. But it's an expensive and labor-intensive process that proper maintenance can eliminate.

Vacuuming stairways. Carpeted stairways need to be vacuumed regularly, right along with the rest of your carpet. The easiest method is to use an upright vacuum, lifting it from stair to stair, and vacuuming the nap thoroughly to get out embedded dirt. The center of the stair gets 90 percent of the abuse. Two or three times a year the corners and edges that cannot be reached with the vacuum can be wiped out with a damp cleaning cloth.

Built-in vacuum systems. A central vac system is a great choice in any new home and brings you one step closer to having a maintenance-free home. The system has lots of power to pull out dirt particles, and it's clean, because residual dust is sucked out of the room. Because the motor is located in the basement or garage, it's also quiet. All you hold is a light hose and handle (easier on the back), and there's no long cord to drag around and get tangled up in or to pull out of the wall plug. And there's no heavy piece of equipment bumping into furniture.

When your carpet reaches the point where cleaning is necessary, have it done professionally. Unlike supermarket rentals, the professionals have

> *People are always daydreaming of the kind of place in which they would like to live, yet never making the place where they do live into anything artistically satisfying to them—always to dream of a rock, glass, and timber house on the cliffs high above the sea while never putting anything of themselves into their small village brick house.*
>
> Edith Schaeffer

the right equipment and expertise needed to get out deeply imbedded soil and solve stain problems. Request a combination of rotary shampoo on heavily soiled areas and steam cleaning overall. After your carpet is cleaned, apply a good soil retardant such as 3M's Carpet Protector. Soil retardants help carpet resist soil and stains and extend the length of time between major cleanings.

Dusting. Dusting is the simplest and easiest way to keep your furniture looking nice. How often you do it depends to a large degree on the air pollution in your area. I live in an agricultural area of California, where dust appears on furniture within an hour after dusting. I've learned to live with it.

Dust is visually offensive to some people's sense of perfection, but it does little physical damage to a home. To reduce dusting to a minimum:

1. Mat each entrance to your home.

2. Empty your vacuum cleaner bag frequently so it doesn't create dust unnecessarily.

3. Properly maintain furnace and air-conditioning filters.

4. Sufficiently weatherproof doors and windows.

When dusting, begin with high places, getting dust and dirt onto the floor, where it can be vacuumed or mopped up easily. It is always best to dust before you vacuum.

Toss out your feather dusters. They do little more than blow particles of dust all over so that you'll still be chasing dust an hour later. A treated dustcloth, available at hardware stores, that picks up dust and leaves no residue is the best way to go. A second choice is a treated paper dustcloth, called Masslin cloth, available at janitorial supply houses. It will last and last, and you can throw the cloth away when it becomes dirt-saturated.

Lamb's wool dusters on the end of a stick are especially good for high places, cobwebs, and venetian or miniblinds. After use, shake dusters outside or vacuum to clean. A dry paintbrush becomes a great dusting

> *One thing I learned early when Jimmy was governor is that you can't dress and have your hair and your fingernails perfect all the time. . . . The house might not be spotless, but he would sit me down and say, "You did the best you could—that's all you can do." You learn that if you're going to do the things you want to do, you can't be perfect; and once you accept that, you can relax.*
>
> ROSALYNN CARTER,
> *PEOPLE* INTERVIEW

tool for lampshades, ornate picture frames, crevices in carved furniture, and other hard-to-clean places, such as computer keyboards and office equipment. The soft bristles whisk dust out of the crevices in seconds.

Polishing. Most homemakers are convinced that the secret to maintaining beautiful wood finishes lies in a bottle or can. They use too much polish, building up layers of gunk and goo. Aerosol polishes should be used seldom and lightly. Since polishes are not always compatible, select one polish and use it consistently. A polish should be chosen on the following merits:

1. Ease of application.
2. Provides lasting protection.
3. Nonsmearing, nonstreaking.
4. Safe for the surface on which it is used.
5. Pleasing scent.
6. Buffs easily.
7. Hides superficial scratches and blemishes.

A water or oil wax emulsion in either aerosol or spray form is a good choice. It protects and enhances wood beauty and is easy to dust. Don't use more frequently than once or twice a year, or eventually layers will build up that will need to be removed. Lemon oil can be used to feed raw or natural wood surfaces in your home.

Bathrooms. Cleaning guru Don Aslett claims that by spending only three and a half minutes per day we should be able to keep our bathrooms in immaculate condition. Whatever our time constraints are, let's learn to do it right.

When cleaning toilets, spray and wipe the entire outside of the toilet, working from top to bottom to avoid transporting the worst concentration of germs toward flushing handles. Remember, it's the outside of the toilet, under the seat, and around the rim that harbors most germs and smells when not cleaned regularly.

For daily maintenance scrub the bowl with a bowl brush. An acid bowl cleaner is actually needed only a couple times per year. If a ring remains, use a pumice stone or "screen," available at hardware stores. Bleach should not be used in the toilet bowl, because it breaks down chrome, formica, and other plastic laminates. Toilet tank capsules that turn the water blue are ineffective, their greatest asset being psychological for those who like blue water. Quick daily maintenance and thorough weekly cleaning are the efficient and smart ways to clean a bathroom.

Next, spray the mirror with window/mirror cleaner. Keep a spray bottle and cleaning cloths in the bathroom for convenient use. Spray the countertops with your bathroom cleaner and let it sit before wiping clean. Now spray the hardware and sink. Use an old toothbrush to clean hardware that is spotted and soiled. Wipe and buff surfaces until they sparkle. Avoid abrasive powdered cleansers on sinks. The abrasive action quickly removes stains, but damages the fiberglass in sinks, tubs, and other fixtures.

A fiberglass shower should be cleaned with your regular disinfectant bathroom cleaner and a white nylon scrub sponge. Do not use abrasive cleaners or scouring pads on fiberglass. Bleach and other harsh solvents can damage the finish. If you clean your shower weekly your bathroom disinfectant should do the trick. The secret is not to let soap scum build up until a small task becomes a major operation. Regular maintenance of the shower/tub area prevents mildew.

If you need a stronger cleanser for a specific problem in your shower, ask for a recommendation at your local janitorial supply house. A good prevention technique for the shower area is a coat of paste wax that will repel scum and hard water buildup. Another prevention technique that I used, even when my children were young, was to require wiping down the shower door/walls with a squeegee or towel. Fifteen seconds of time spent here saves hours of hard labor later.

Last of all, drop to your knees. Spray the floor with your disinfectant spray and wipe clean with a cleaning cloth. Unless your bathroom exceeds 15 to 20 square feet, this is faster than fumbling with a mop, fetching a bucket, mixing cleaning solution, and attempting to maneuver around all those bathroom fixtures in a small area.

Your bathroom is now clean. Stand back and admire. Light a candle, place a rose in a bud vase on the counter, or spray a scented spray before you leave. Take pride in what has been accomplished in record time.

Cleaning appliances. It's much better to maintain your oven and refrigerator consistently rather than letting them go for years between cleanings. After lengthy periods these tasks become major depressing and time-consuming chores.

Use a heavy-duty, all-purpose cleaning solution for enamel, stainless steel, or plastic surfaces. Avoid using abrasive scouring cleansers, metal scrapers, steel wool, or nylon scouring pads on appliances, as they can be damaging.

Stoves. A general rule for cleaning stoves and other difficult-to-clean areas is to spend more time soaking and less time scrubbing. Spray the surface to be cleaned with your heavy-duty cleaning solution and let it sit for a few minutes. Then use a tough Chore Girl-type cleaning pad, soaked with cleaning solution, to remove the caked-on grease and dirt. Wipe clean with a soft cloth.

Ovens. Unless you have a self-cleaning oven, all ovens are cleaned in much the same way—a lot of elbow grease. Apply a brand-name oven cleaner, wait for the chemicals to loosen the spills and spatters, and then scrub off what is still left with a Chore Girl pad. Be sure to wear rubber gloves to protect your hands from the chemicals, and open the windows for proper ventilation against strong fumes.

Window cleaning. Most homemakers dread all the climbing, reaching, and stretching involved in cleaning windows. Then, just when they think they are finished, they step back to view their handiwork. The angle of the sun has changed, and streaks, smudges, and wipe marks appear for all the world to see.

The main reason windows and mirrors appear streaked is because of the stuff that's put on them. A waxy layer of polish builds up every time you clean the window, creating a more difficult cleaning situation. The polish smeared on the window also creates a surface more likely to attract and hold dust, dirt, and airborne particles. The result is windows that need to be cleaned more frequently.

Your windows can gleam again, but not if you continue to clean them as you have in the past. Dump all archaic ideas involving newspaper and paper towels. Dump all window cleaning supplies in your cupboard.

> *Why not surround yourself now with things that communicate something of your appreciation, taste, and interests. . . . Why not express yourself in your choice of things you can produce yourself? There is great satisfaction in making something out of nothing.*
>
> Edith Schaeffer

Without a backward glance, toss into the garbage forever every container of glass and mirror polish and wax that you have been using for years and prepare your own window-cleaning solution. Resist the tendency to add more detergent or ammonia. It isn't necessary and can actually streak your windows and leave a residue. For big jobs where a bucket is needed, use one gallon of water, four tablespoons of ammonia, and eight to 10 drops of liquid dish soap.

Cleaning windows requires using the right equipment. Buy yourself one important and efficient window-cleaning tool—a professional-quality brass or stainless steel squeegee, found at a janitorial supply house or a good hardware store. (Ettore Steccone brand is perhaps the best.) Now you are prepared to have clean windows in five steps:

Step 1: Spray the window, or wet the window lightly with your prepared window cleaner solution, using a clean sponge or wand applicator. Avoid drowning the window in solution. If it's really dirty, or has years of spots and residue on it, go over the area again.

Step 2: Wipe the squeegee blade with a damp chamois or cloth to moisten it. A dry blade will bump and skip as you wipe the window; a damp blade will glide along.

Step 3: Squeegee across the top first. Tilt the squeegee at an angle to the top of the window so that the edge of the squeegee next to the sill presses in, and the rest of the squeegee rests lightly on the glass. Now pull the squeegee across the window. By doing this first you prevent drips from running down from the top.

Step 4: Place your squeegee at the top of the window and pull down. With each pull, go back to the dry area at the top of the window and begin again, overlapping into the dry, clean area. Wipe the blade with your chamois or cloth after each stroke.

Step 5: Finish with a horizontal stroke across the bottom to remove water that may have puddled there.

Presto! Perfect windows!

The squeegee method is almost as easy as it sounds. If you don't succeed with the squeegee your first try, try again. Squeegees are a little difficult for first-time users to handle. But a little practice makes perfect. It may also take a little time to dissolve the accumulation of dirt layered on your windows. After a couple cleanings, however, the previous accumulation of stuff should be removed. If the squeegee blade starts to leave a line of solution on your windows, pull the blade out, turn it over, and snap it back in. When the blade wears out entirely, buy a new blade and snap it into the blade holder.

Occasionally I need the assistance of housecleaners. As they enter my house I request that they leave all their cleaning solutions, polishes, and paraphernalia outside and use mine. I take them to my cleaning center and begin instructions on which product to use. One of these women was so impressed with my window cleaner that she exclaimed, "What is this stuff? It doesn't streak. It works like magic!"

Hardwater buildup on windows from automatic sprinkling systems requires a mild professional phosphoric acid cleaner. Then adjust your sprinkling system.

Blinds. No matter how you cut it, blinds are a pain. I knew that before I installed miniblinds in five rooms of my house. I hate them, but can't live without them. They are attractive and allow the adjustment of light into a room, but they are bears to clean!

What's the best way to clean a bear? Regular maintenance. Close the miniblind. With your lamb's wool duster, thoroughly sweep one flat side of the blind. Then move to the other side. Now close the blind in the opposite direction and repeat the process. The entire blind is now dusted.

Cleaning windows requires using the right equipment. . . . The squeegee method is almost as easy as it sounds.

Over time, without regular maintenance, blinds collect dust and residue that can build up and not come off with dusting. The experts say to remove the blinds from the window, take them outside, and lay them on an old quilt or piece of canvas. Close the louvers and scrub with a soft-bristle brush, using an all-purpose cleaner. I tried this once and will never do it again. It was an exhausting ordeal.

Even though it is time-consuming, once in a while I wet-clean the blinds, louver by louver, with a cleaning cloth. Rather than scheduling time to do this, I wait for a time when I get a long-winded phone call, then head for the blind that needs cleaning, portable phone in hand. A couple phone calls like this and I can have a clean miniblind. Regular maintenance prevents having to do this often.

A Word to Perfectionists

Discussions of housecleaning throw perfectionists into a tizzy. Perfectionism, as we are using it here, is the need to be perfect and do everything perfectly. Contrary to what some people think, perfectionism is not a virtue. It doesn't mean you are perfect or that you think you are. The perfectionist is never able to turn her desire-to-be-perfect switch off.

Ginny typifies what we're talking about. She is driven to be *the best* at everything she tackles—wife, mother, homemaker, teacher, and hostess. "No matter how stressed I am with my full-time teaching or with the children, the house always has to be perfect," she explained. "I can't let anything go."

When planning to entertain, she begins weeks ahead. Every minute detail must be perfect—the menu, table setting, house, kids, furniture. She thinks if she gets everything perfect she can relax. It never works that way. The need to be perfect is robbing Ginny of enjoying the event.

Ginny and all other perfectionists not only drive themselves crazy by obsessing over details, but they rear like-minded children. A mother who is compelled to redo a daughter's attempt at making her bed comes across as critical and difficult to please, affecting the child's self-esteem. The child senses that she never measures up to her parents' expectations for her. She may end up feeling loved and valued only when she performs in a perfect manner.

The drive for perfection can be self-defeating in another way. It takes perfectionists forever to get anything done. They have a need to improve and polish every detail repeatedly, regardless of how inconsequential. As a result they wind up organizing two drawers meticulously rather than giving the entire house a much-needed once-over. Perfectionists are often master procrastinators when it comes to housecleaning or any other tasks. Because they can accept nothing short of absolute perfection, every cleaning project looms impossibly large. Perfectionists are also often reluctant to try new things. As beginners at any task, they will likely not be good at it. Unrealistically high expectations are bad enough when one has them only for oneself, but perfectionism is a trait that doesn't set well with others. Imposition of exceptionally high standards affects all these interpersonal relationships—spouses, children, coworkers, and employees

A perfectionist I am not! On a scale of 1 to 10 I try to maintain a 7 or 8. I could maintain a 9 or 10 (I think). But being the happy, sanguine person I am, having fun with friends often supersedes housecleaning tasks.

If you identified with Ginny and know you are a perfectionist, or lean in that direction, ease up gradually. When this concept was brought to one woman's attention, she said, "I began to realize that keeping the house a perfect 10 all the time was preventing me from doing many of the things in life I want to do." Later she confessed, "Now the house isn't as neat and clean, but I'm having a lot more fun."

If just saying you'll ease up doesn't work for you, you can give yourself a deadline for getting a job done and meet it, regardless. Should you get sidetracked by trying to perfect every detail on a certain task, establish a time limit. Say to yourself, "You have a half hour to complete the vacuuming. Now move it!"

Should you find yourself making negative critical judgments about yourself, another technique is necessary. Negative self-talk can be replaced with positive self-talk. Every time a negative thought crosses your brain, replace it with a positive one. For example, when you fail to meet a deadline, say, "I can learn to meet my deadlines and complete tasks on schedule" instead of "I never get anything done on time. I'm hopeless!"

Break large tasks into smaller ones, especially when a task appears overwhelming. Rather than attempting to wash all the windows in the entire house, break the job into manageable portions. Complete two windows per week rather than attempting to do all windows and feeling as if you failed because you finished only two. Recognize that if your home has 10 windows, with such a plan all your windows could be clean in five weeks. Yes, it took five weeks, but you completed the task. This is much better than feeling you failed.

Isn't it time you cut yourself—and others—a little slack?

Cleaning Services

Some women need encouragement—even permission—to hire a cleaning service. So here it is:

> *I, Nancy Van Pelt, do hereby both encourage and give you permission to hire a cleaning service when necessary to bring your home under control and gain peace of mind.*

When "clean" gets neglected at our house for two to three weeks at a time because I've been on an extensive travel itinerary, I need help. What I appreciate about Harry is the encouragement he gives me to call a cleaning service when I feel it's necessary. I'm easier to live with when "clean" is caught up in my home, and I have more time for him. We both benefit from a cleaning service.

A reliable cleaning service is not easy to find. Ask your friends for recommendations. Narrow your choices down to three and begin making calls. I asked several services to come to my home, where I interviewed them and got estimates. This is an important decision. You will be allowing strangers to enter your home and handle your most precious possessions. Your housecleaners will see the most intimate areas of your home. If they are irresponsible, they could break or steal valuables. Choose a cleaning service with a reputation for honesty and reliability.

Most services will attempt to lock you into a regular weekly or biweekly service. I couldn't afford this, nor did I want this much help. I had to interview several services until I found one that would clean on call. The help comes by twos or threes. I take the women's names so I can ask for them again if I like them, or can request others if they don't work out. Another one of my requirements is that they use the cleaning products I provide.

I hire help maybe once every one to three months, depending on my schedule. But having the freedom to call on a cleaning service as needed, when I am beginning to "lose it," is another of my secrets to sanity!

When they arrive, we do a walk-through of each room, and I tell them what I want done. If they haven't cleaned for me before, I give them a written list of what is required in each room. Before they leave I do another walk-through to check if everything has been done. I rotate thoroughness of tasks for them also. Remember, the service is hired by you and they must please you, their customer. You don't want to be demanding or unreasonable, but they should accomplish what you want them to, as long as it fits under their job description.

I hire help maybe once every one to three months, depending on my schedule. But having the freedom to call on a cleaning service as needed, when I am beginning to "lose it," is another of my secrets to sanity!

Housekeeping Standards

Housekeeping standards should adjust to the varying stages of the family life cycle. In early marriage household duties remain relatively easy, as each partner pitches in and carries his or her share. When infants and young children enter the scene, the household tasks so easily cared for and shared before babies escalate overnight into major, seemingly never-ending tasks. As the children grow, the total number of hours spent on housekeeping increases. Children may offer helping hands, but it requires a great deal of time and patience to make sure children complete their tasks well. You may discover that teenagers may want an orderly, well-maintained home but are unwilling to contribute time or energy toward accomplishing this goal.

During empty-nest years household chores become infinitely less complicated as your household resumes a less hectic schedule, similar to that of early marriage before children. Standards for an orderly home must be balanced against the current needs and interests of your family during the various stages.

A Clean Home Has Its Rewards

You now know how to maintain a care-less home and keep it that way. But since no robot has yet been invented to do your housework, you'll still either have to do it yourself or hire it done. But you now know the best ways for getting it done in record time. You may discover mundane realities to housecleaning. Every job has them, and housework is no exception. Expect it, and handle it with class.

Cleanliness is important, but it isn't the most important thing in the world. There is merit in maintaining a clean home and in performing your tasks in a manner befitting a woman of excellence. But let's not become slaves to cleaning routines. It's possible to maintain a clean house at an acceptable level of cleanliness and save a lot of time, energy, and discouragement.

Clean Like a Pro

Assignments:
1. Begin to clean like a pro. Purchase the proper cleaning supplies and equipment. Place good mats at every entrance, and teach your family prevention techniques for keeping dirt out.
2. Stop doing and begin delegating!
3. For personal devotions read Ephesians 5:15, 16: "Look carefully then how you walk—not as unwise [women] but as wise, making the most of the time, because the days are evil" (RSV).

These verses say to me: _____

_____

_____

As a result of what these verses tell me, I will _____

_____

_____

Hard work is not stressful.
Losing control over your life is.

AFFIRMATION
for Secret to Sanity 6

*T*oday I choose to put order in my life. I no longer fear failure. I can clearly see myself functioning successfully and happily on this day. I am grateful that I have a home to clean. Lord, grant me purpose and strength to clean my home. It can be done, and it can be fun!

Lift your spirits—go the extra mile

1. When you begin to feel overwhelmed, take a break from whatever is causing you stress and attend to some task that will please and bring you instant gratification. Then you can go back to your previous task with renewed energy.
2. Before going to sleep tonight, lie in bed and think about one thing you did well today. Congratulate yourself. Build on today's success for tomorrow.
3. The next time you hear your favorite vocalist singing, sing along too. This can lift your spirits. Sing a happy song and send a happy message to others.

---

*If not available, try Maintenance One All-purpose cleaner M-11, available at True Value, Coast to Coast, and Servstar hardware stores.

†If not available, try Maintenance One Concentrated Germicidal cleaner M-12, available at True Value, Coast to Coast, and Servstar hardware stores.

*Find a time and place that you and
your family can talk with few interruptions.*

8

CHORE WARS:

TACTICS FOR GETTING HUSBANDS AND KIDS TO HELP

ituation: The clothes hamper is overflowing. Your husband and/or children would:

    a. Throw shirts at the hamper anyway, and leave them on the floor if they should miss.

b. Shout, "Honey/Mom, you forgot to do the wash!"

c. Not even notice an overflowing hamper.

d. Do the laundry if you asked.

e. Understand that doing laundry is their responsibility.

Even if your response is a, b, or c, don't give up hope! When a woman works outside the home *and* has a family to care for, she has two jobs. This takes a toll on women, their marriages, and their children. With more and more women working outside the home, there may be a revolution going on in the workplace, but at home it's business as usual. Women continue to carry a far greater portion of homemaking tasks and child rearing responsibilities than their male counterparts.

In a family without children, the home generally remains low maintenance. The husband likely does less, and the wife accepts this. Or she may demand more, and he'll pitch in a little, but neither tampers much with accepted traditional roles.

But when a couple has children, smoldering issues arise. Two-career family life may run smoothly on television sitcoms, but a different picture emerges in real life. In real life women are stressed-out, cross, irritable. They feed their families fast foods, are too exhausted to make love, get behind in all their housework, send their kids to day care (even when they are sick), neglect their husbands and children—and feel guilty.

The Second Shift

Sociologist Arlie Hohschild studied 150 two-career couples to find out what happened when they returned home from work. The results were published in his book *The Second Shift*. The total number of hours each parent spent at his or her job, doing household chores, and taking care of children were added up. Hohschild's research showed that women get 20 to 25 minutes less sleep per night than their husbands, who get a full seven to eight hours. Mothers of children under 3 years of age do even worse. They get 45 to 50 minutes less sleep per night. Total this up for a week, and you see that Mom misses almost one whole night of sleep every week. The lack of sleep and the resulting tiredness takes its toll on women and their families. According to Hohschild, women sometimes talk about sleep the way a starving person talks about food.

> *At a certain point I realized . . . there are things you can give up without giving up being a "good mother."*
>
> MARGO BERK-LEVINE, EMPLOYMENT AGENCY OWNER

This study also found that husbands had 15 more hours of free time per week than their wives. Over a year this amounts to a month of free time to do what they wish while their wives raise the children and clean house.

In most families men resisted any efforts at changing the status quo and taking over any major responsibilities. (I can certainly understand why!) Although different studies turn up varying results, most white-collar men normally do about 5 percent of household chores. Blue-collar men may do as much as 20 percent. For women who work full-time outside the home and have to do it all, this spells burnout and stress.

The picture is clear: Women fight for change. Men resist. The result? Women close themselves off emotionally from their husbands. Hohschild observed that the men in the study were forfeiting something vital to the health, and possibly even the survival, of their marriage—namely, the love and respect of their wives. Although the women in the study were maintaining the extra load, one thing happened over which they had little control: they were closing down emotionally. Eventually anger and resentment emerge and constantly smolder beneath the surface. Men don't understand the phenomenon. They sense something is wrong in their relationship but don't know what.

When a man contributes his part around the house, research states it is vitally connected to his wife's sense of being loved. Men see no connection between the two. Their ever-loving wives are slipping away from them emotionally, and the men don't even know it!

Behind the breezy facade of every superwoman is likely hiding a stressed-out, resentful woman, or one who is headed in that direction. It all stems from the issue of "Who'll do the housework?"

One mom suffered from constant fatigue. She worked as a nurse practitioner in a busy office. Every day she returned home and cooked nutritious meals, dutifully cleaned the house, paid the bills on time, and did the laundry and shopping on schedule. In other words, *she did it all*. But one day exhaustion took over. She totally collapsed and simply could not move.

After a doctor's visit and some much-needed rest, she recognized that changes had to be made. She gathered her husband and children for an urgent meeting and presented a list of chores that had to be completed weekly. Each was instructed to choose what they wished to do to help. Mom planned a week's menu and assigned out grocery shopping, table setting, cleanup, and three meals a week. She turned the checkbook over to her husband. That was 15 years ago. Although the original plan has been modified repeatedly, it works.

It is mandatory, not to mention scriptural, that husbands and children assist with household tasks. Paul asks us to "bear one another's burdens" (Gal. 6:2, RSV). I believe that includes how we live together at home. It means that husbands, wives, and children must work together to maintain common living space.

Creative Ideas for Getting Help

Here are a few creative ideas that can be put to use quickly and easily without major trauma to anyone:

1. *Initiate a family cleanup hour.* According to Don Aslett, 38 percent of housework has nothing to do with cleaning. Instead, it deals with clutter—putting everything away. To solve this problem, call all family

members together for one hour every week to put belongings away and tidy up the house.

Three things make this work: a. Everyone takes part (even Dad). Everyone works together, or not at all. b. Everyone works in teams. No one tackles a mess alone, even though only one person may have made it. While a daughter straightens her room, Dad vacuums. While Mom sorts through the clutter on top of the refrigerator, a son mops the kitchen floor. c. No one stops or plays until either the work is done or 60 minutes is up—whichever comes first.

2. Take five minutes for pickup. All family members (including Mom) take five minutes to tidy up before leaving their rooms in the morning. Make it a rule: Before coming to breakfast, hang up your towel, put your brush away, and make your bed. Just five minutes. Be firm, consistent, and reasonable. And stay with it.

No parent should perform maid service for other adults or children who are old enough to go to school. Insist that family members pick up after themselves. If they fail to cooperate or "forget," start a buy-back basket. You pick up the item, and they buy it back for 25 cents (or a dollar, if you get desperate). Keep the money and treat yourself to a surprise. You earned it!

3. Post a list of jobs. People who don't ask for help rarely get it, especially if that pattern has been learned through prior experience by living in a family in which good ole Mom does everything. Why should anyone put anything away or become responsible when Mom does it for them? Those raised in such families learn to *expect* someone else to pick up, put away, and become responsible.

When Mom gets sick and tired of being everyone else's servant, she'll find that written messages work wonders. Post a list of jobs to be done in a message center. This eliminates "I didn't know," "I forgot," and other excuses. Every once in a while, provide a surprise or a reward. This keeps everyone reading the list, and it makes doing chores worthwhile.

4. Switch roles temporarily. A friend told me that as her husband was about to leave the house one morning he turned to her and said, "You're so lucky to get to stay home all day in this lovely home and this beautiful setting. I really envy you." She was floored. On this day her To Do list was 20 items long. The pressure on her was incredible before her day even began. Every minute would be spent running errands, chauffeuring children, and getting household tasks completed. Her husband had little or no understanding of what she handled daily or the kind of pressure she was under.

A temporary switching of roles under such circumstances can work wonders. Talk your husband into a role switch for two or three days, or even a week, if you can get away with it. You do the tasks he ordinarily does. Your tasks become his responsibility. Being exposed to the reality of a spouse's world for a week can be a real eye-opener. After two days of this, one husband observed, "I'm not doing as much as I thought I was, and she's doing more than her share." Once husband and wife fully experience the other's world of responsibility at home, each may be more open to negotiating change.

5. Go on strike. If you have tried all these ideas and nothing works, and you are getting desperate for help, go on strike. Leave beds unmade, clothes and towels on the floor, wet clothes in the washer, dry clothes in the dryer, and dishes on the table. Let your family know you can't do it all anymore. Put up a sign on the front lawn that says *This mom is on strike!* Let your family know there will be no meals until the kitchen is cleaned up and that the kids can get to no activities until you get full cooperation. Then stay on strike until your family is willing to negotiate a plan for sharing household tasks.

This worked for Nadine, who was married and had two teenage sons. She handled most household responsibilities, but since she worked outside the home full-time, she asked one thing of the three men in her life when she began preparing dinner: that the garbage be emptied, all dishes be put into the dishwasher, and everything on the decks be put away. This was rarely done. She had alternately pleaded, screamed, and begged. Nothing worked. That's when she decided to go on strike.

> *Delegating is the best thing in the world you can do for yourself.*
>
> VICKI RIKER,
> MEDIA DIRECTOR

The next time she found the kitchen dirty, she went to the family room, turned on the television, and sat down to quilt. Her husband and sons wanted to know why she wasn't preparing supper. "I don't cook in a dirty kitchen," she replied pleasantly. No blaming; no judging; just a statement of fact. The men exchanged looks and disappeared into the kitchen. A few minutes later they emerged, proclaiming it clean and ready for inspection. Nadine cheerfully went to cook supper. This worked wonders for a couple nights before she found it messy again. She went back on strike, watching TV and quilting, while the men went to the kitchen. If you decide to go on strike, be consistent. Every time your conditions are not met, strike until you get what you must have.

6. *Use rewards wisely.* Make helping with chores pay off. Offer rewards after specific tasks are completed. "Just as soon as these Legos, toys, and clothes are picked up, you can call John and go to the park to play ball." "As soon as you get the lawn mowed, you can play a computer game." "If you get that entire row of vegetables weeded in the next half hour, I have a special treat for you." "Make sure as you dust that you lift up each object and do the job thoroughly, because I've hidden some money that's yours to keep for helping me on this busy day."

7. *Make it fun to work together.* Make chores pleasant and fun. When a parent criticizes, nags, and complains, the family develops negative attitudes toward work. Children work better when someone works with them. Working together in the yard, for example, with each person doing a different task, provides great opportunities for togetherness, communication, teaching, sharing, and playing. The same technique can be used when cleaning the garage or house. Find things to laugh about. Add a song, tell a story, listen to music, whistle. Afterward, play a game together, have a water fight, or head for the park. Exercise a little creativity and the family will learn that work can be fun. What's learned with pleasure is learned full measure.

> *There are three ways to get something done: do it yourself, hire someone to do it, or forbid your children to do it.*
>
> ANONYMOUS

The previous suggestions work well with children *and* husbands. Husbands respond to rewards as well as do children. Let your husband know that if he does his part you'll have more time to spend with him. Let him know you won't be so tired and cranky, and that you'll be more interested in, and have more energy for, an intimate sexual interlude. Tell him that pitching in willingly and taking responsibility off your shoulders will pay big dividends.

8. *Appreciate and praise effectively.* Both men and children respond favorably to sincere appreciation and lavish praise when offered appropriately. You may even discover that family members will deliberately tackle tasks just to win praise. Make it worth their effort. Effective praise provides motivation to do it again. A sincere compliment is always appreciated.

Negotiating for Change
Let's say you've tried the quick-and-easy ways previously mentioned

to get some help. Nothing works. You analyze what's going on in your home: You clean the entire house. He washes the car. You cook a meal. He dries the car. You see the kids through a parent-teacher conference. He polishes the car. You run errands, chauffeuring kids to the pediatrician, dentist, orthodontist, and music lessons, grocery shopping, going to the post office, banking, and taking shoes to be repaired. He vacuums the car. He calls you to bring him a roll of toilet paper or a glass of water and expects you to know where his keys, glasses, nail clippers, wallet, work shirt, pen, and Swiss Army knife have gone. Although you are up to your wrists in preparing spaghetti, the kids are screaming for a Band-Aid, and the dog is coughing up something extremely unattractive on the living room rug. When the phone rings he calls to you from his comfy chair in front of the television: "Can you get that, hon?"

You both earn the money, but the division of responsibilities around your house is fuzzy and seems tipped unfairly in your direction. Granted, you went into marriage understanding you were entering a world of give-and-take. But nothing prepared you for give, and give, and give some more. So you wind up doing things for everyone else in the family—things they could do for themselves. Saying "Get it yourself, honey" or "Clean up after making a mess" or "You can answer the phone as easily as I" takes more time, energy, and fortitude than you can muster. You find it easier and less stressful to do it yourself.

The previous suggestions may provide temporary relief, but what about the long haul? One survey of 22,000 homes revealed that 43 percent of husbands helped their wives, but only when asked.[1] One woman explained, "I appreciate a helping hand, but what I really want is to be able to count on specific jobs being shared and completed weekly . . . that every week he would vacuum, every morning he would make the bed, every Wednesday night he would fix a meal or shop for groceries."

Getting permanent change over the long haul requires change in the family system. Such change requires negotiation and discussion. Before an important discussion like this, consider these pointers on the art of negotiation:

1. Find a quiet place to talk. Find a time and place that you and your spouse can talk with few interruptions—after the children are in bed, or over dinner in a restaurant. Discussion in a public setting is a good idea, especially if you fear losing control. It forces you to control volume, personal attacks, and nonverbals.

2. Say it straight. State feelings openly and respectfully through the effective use of "I" messages. "I feel overwhelmed by the amount of tasks that I have to do every evening when I come home from work." "Angry" may best describe your feelings, but to say "I feel angry when you aren't helping around the house" may not get the point across as well as other, more specific, *feeling* words such as "upset," "exasperated," "annoyed," "resentful," or "frustrated." Speak calmly. Lower your volume rather than raising it.

3. *Describe what you are experiencing.* Explain clearly, in nonblaming terms, the effect of overload on you, the marriage, the children. Specifically, this may include lack of sleep, continual tiredness, and lack of time for church, friends, hobbies, or recreation. The clearer the picture, the better he'll understand.

4. *Stay with the subject.* Side issues may surface, but stay with the subject of how the housework will get done. The more problems that surface, the less likely you'll solve any of them.

5. *Show respect.* No matter how unhappy you are with the current level of task sharing, you can still show respect. Here are some no-no's:

No name-calling: "You act like a slob."

No remarks about in-laws or relatives: "You are lazier than your father, and he's the laziest I've ever seen!"

No put-downs: "The trouble with you is you are just plain sloppy."

6. *Offer concrete solutions.* Once feelings have been aired constructively, encourage him to offer suggestions. But you'd better have some tangible and creative solutions to offer too. For example, five minutes of picking up before children leave for school or go to bed; a family cleanup hour; posting a list of jobs for everyone to do daily, etc. Be specific, but don't push too hard.

7. *Evaluate the solutions.* Once all available information has been aired and suggestions for solutions laid on the table, together consider choices about a course of action most likely to succeed. When we are anxious to negotiate change, our tendency is to fill each pause or hesitation with words and push, push, push. Try to be comfortable with silences, especially if he is quieter than you.

8. *Really listen.* Get a clear picture of his views and ideas. Sometimes it's helpful to paraphrase: "Let me see if I understand correctly. You feel . . ." This allows you to see if your own perceptions are correct and gives the opportunity for him to hear again what has been said.[2]

9. *Choose an acceptable solution.* Good solutions can be reached when both parties compromise. Winning is not the goal. Where there is a

winner, there must also be a loser—and no one likes to lose. Once you come to an agreement, bring the subject up during a family conference and involve the children in the problem-solving process.

10. Implement the decision. Decide who is to do what, where, and when. Consider who has more time, expertise, concern, and enjoyment for each task, and then decide who will do it. Jotting down what each person has agreed to handle avoids misunderstandings later.

11. Hang in there! At times we may be tempted to say "Forget it. I'll do it alone." Don't. We often leave unpleasant situations too soon when we could, within minutes, reach a solution. If the first plan you negotiate fails, go back to the drawing board and renegotiate until everyone accepts responsibility. Even workable plans need to be adjusted and negotiated as children grow and mature, people move in and out of the home, family needs change, or when a family moves to a new home.

Whatever the circumstance, refuse to become your family's maid service and servant.

After Negotiation

After negotiation, especially if we've experienced conflict, we need reassurance that we are loved and cared for. Find something positive on which to comment. Give an unexpected compliment, a pat on the back, a hug, a kiss, or a big smile. These things draw us closer again.

All of us respond positively to appreciation and often try to win further approval. Harry noticed how extremely tired I was the other day and offered to fix the meal. I was openly enthusiastic over his efforts. When I bragged about the meal later to our friends, I overheard him say, "If it means this much to her, I'll do it again." Appreciation is a powerful motivator in changing behavior. Instead of criticizing when others fail to help, comment favorably when they do. This is called positive reinforcement.

Friendly negotiation can solve chore war conflicts. Be patient with yourself, your spouse, and your children. Change doesn't take place overnight. New habits take time to establish. Don't expect too much too soon. Pray, then keep asking. Homes in which family members do their fair share are happier.

---

[1] Margery D. Rosen, "The American Mother," *Ladies' Home Journal,* May 1990, p. 132.

[2] For further help on how to listen, talk, and resolve conflict, readers may wish to consult my book *How to Talk So Your Mate Will Listen and Listen So Your Mate Will Talk* (Grand Rapids: Baker Books, 1989).

Enjoyable leisure must be planned for, especially if the objective of destressing our lives is to be realized.

9

SECRET TO SANITY 7:

TIME-OUT FOR SIMPLE PLEASURE!

aron Carlson is married and the mother of two grade school children. She begins each day at 6:00, when she drags herself out of bed and into the shower. By 6:30 she gets the girls up and supervises their morning routine, as well as her husband's. By 7:30 she's out the door, drops the children off at school, and heads for her office, where she begins her full-time job. At 5:00 that afternoon Caron picks up the girls from their after-school baby-sitter and is home by 5:45, beginning her evening marathon of cooking dinner, bathing children, checking book bags, packing lunch boxes, and laying out clothes for the next day. Sometime between 9:30 and 11:30, after dinner cleanup and a load or two of laundry, she collapses.

If you ask her what she'd like to do in her spare time, she'd roll her eyes and chortle, "What free time?" If you pressed her for a response, she'd say, "I'd love to take oil painting lessons, work out at the gym, or go antiquing, but I don't know where I'd squeeze such luxuries into my packed schedule."

Is Caron stressed? Yes. Is her life horrible? Not exactly. For Caron and thousands of others in their 30s and 40s, attempting to achieve family and career goals all at once is quite normal. Their lives are busy as they marry and combine child rearing with career launching. But there is also tremendous potential for overload. The goal for women is to find a balance in which life is rich without slipping into the area in which one's responsibilities become overwhelming.

Time Is at a Premium

Time is always at a premium for women, but especially for women in their 30s and 40s. According to a *Ladies' Home Journal* survey, more than 50 percent of the women in this age group feel stressed out, at least occasionally, while 22 percent said they often felt that way. The biggest source of stress, they agreed, was not having enough hours in the day to accomplish everything they needed to do.[1]

Another survey of more than 1,000 Americans, conducted by Hilton Hotels Corporation, found that during an average weekend people between the ages of 30 and 49 spend roughly nine hours more than they want to on chores.

There is always time to do the things you really want to do.

ANONYMOUS

Having a demanding schedule isn't all bad. When you have a seemingly endless list of obligations to meet, it provides motivation to achieve, to keep going, and to use effective problem-solving skills. The more challenges one takes on, the more one can accomplish and the more gratifying life can become.

It isn't good or healthy, however, to have pressure every hour of every day. It is essential to incorporate personal time into one's schedule, even during the most hectic years. Women yearn to engage in some fun activities for their own personal enjoyment, but tend to give this last priority. As a woman's roles pile up and her responsibilities compound, extra time becomes nonexistent. Research shows that women are 21 minutes short every day of time needed to complete everything they'd like. As a result, they end up overscheduling themselves and doing two or more things at a time.

"I don't even get six hours of sleep every night," a superexhausted woman muttered under her breath. "Now you expect me to add one more thing to my To Do list!"

Allow me to ask a question. Do you want to just "exist" and barely survive each day? Or would you like to experience happiness and life to its fullest today?

Women Have Less Time for Leisure

Juliet B. Schor, associate professor of economics at Harvard University, reported in her book *The Overworked American: The Unexpected Decline of Leisure* that people in the United States have been working longer hours but allowing themselves *less time to play!* Schor says that employed women who are also mothers average more than 80 hours per week in housework, child care, and employment, but only 16½ hours per week in leisure time activities.

According to a Harris poll, access to free time has fallen 40 percent in the past two decades. This should not surprise us, since within the same time frame the number of hours the average American works in a year increased by a whopping 138. And, Schor notes, women feel the greatest time squeeze of all. When annual hours of paid employment in all industry and occupations were compared over a 20-year period, she estimates, "Men are working nearly 100 more hours per year—or an extra two and a half weeks—while women are putting in about 300 more hours—which translates into an extra seven and a half weeks."[2] What's more, paid time off (vacation and sick leave) for Americans has been simultaneously shrinking, falling 15 percent in the 1980s.

When a woman works too much, she may forget how to relax and have fun. Abandoning the pressures of the rat race to which she's become accustomed makes her feel uncomfortable and guilty. Guilt may be the number one spoilsport that prevents women from enjoying life. When a woman is faced with a block of free time and nothing specific to do, her mind churns out the "I shoulds." I should do a load of laundry . . . organize the hall closet . . . catch up on mending . . . paint the bathroom.

Many women simply don't feel entitled to enjoy leisure activities. The concept of leisure time is elusive because, unlike men, women have no clear delineation between work and home. While some men pitch in with household tasks at home, free time for most of them is what is left once work is over. For women, however, there's plenty more to do at home after work. And because women carry more responsibilities, they rarely have the block of free time men enjoy.

What's more, women have been socially conditioned to be caretakers. Consequently, many women not only nurture their husbands and children, they also take over nurturing bosses and coworkers, neighbors and friends. Only rarely do women take time to nurture themselves.

Burnout Ahead!

This all-work-and-no-play mind-set quickly leads to burnout. Women must learn to give themselves permission to break away from their endless list of role expectations to pursue their own leisure activities. It will never happen until women take it upon themselves to make leisure time a priority. In some cases a woman may need to go one step further—be assertive enough to make sure those around her also see it as a priority.

Some women prefer work to play. Why? They operate in continuous overdrive, because work is the only area in which they feel truly competent. Or a woman may choose this route because she's stuck in a poor marriage, or wants to be married but isn't. So she works until she drops—puts in overtime, brings work home, takes on extra projects—all to sustain the feeling of competence and control.

Doing it makes a woman feel indispensable, providing another boost to her self-esteem. So a woman may complain and bemoan the tremendous pressure she's under, and resist letting go because being indispensable reassures her that she is valuable and needed. Such workaholic behavior can not only become addictive and add loads of unnecessary stress to a woman's life, but also prevent her from enjoying leisure time. Whereas productive employment and selfless nurturing boosts self-esteem, it cannot resolve the issue of too much work and no play.

According to Diane Fassel, Ph.D., author of *Working Ourselves to Death: The High Cost of Workaholism, the Rewards of Recovery*, work cannot give us identity. It cannot make us happy. And when we expect work to do things for us that we are not willing to do for ourselves, we become exhausted."[3]

The good news is that leisure activities, when chosen wisely, can and do offer increased self-esteem and a sense of fulfillment. Research indicates that a proper balance between leisure and work complement each other. Creative insight usually occurs during periods of relaxation, not during peak effort.

Leisure 101: A Crash Course

When we were going through school, most of us turned to counselors who assisted with the selection of courses that would help us reach our educational and occupational goals. We may have even taken tests that measured our aptitude, skills, ability, and interest for entering our chosen area of life work. Yet few of us would ever think of applying such an approach to pursuing leisure activities. Actually, planning leisure is an unfamiliar concept to many. Most people expect wonderful things to happen during free time with minimal or no planning. It doesn't happen that way.

Enjoyable leisure must be planned for, especially if the objective of de-stressing our lives is to be realized.

So how can a woman cut down on stress overload, put balance back into her life, and get some personal time? Here's some ideas that will help you get started.

1. Readjust your attitude. Recognize that taking time for yourself is not something you should be doing only if it's convenient, you can find the time, work it into your schedule, or afford it. You must begin thinking of time for yourself as a priority, not a luxury item. If you don't begin taking care of some of your needs, you won't be of much help to others. Taking time for yourself will refresh you, energize your spirits, lessen your stress, and make your efforts at handling multiple priorities more successful.

2. Make a date with yourself. Schedule personal time on your calendar just as you would a board meeting, piano lessons, or a dental appointment. Unless you do, your time will get crowded out with chores or other responsibilities. Health is maintained not by decreasing the amount of stress in your life, but by adding relaxation, fun, and/or downtime to your schedule. And for a woman who is handling multiple priorities, this means making it a priority by scheduling it on a calendar.

> *Leisure is as good for you as vitamins or sleep. If it will help you to kick the guilt habit, look at it this way: You owe it to your work, your family, and yourself.*
> KATE RAND LLOYD
> EDITOR, WORKING WOMAN

Every week as I turn the page of my daily planner to face a new week, I write in my Jazzercize class, my Tuesday and Thursday destressor. These two weekly appointments take priority over everything else. Jazzercize is something I truly enjoy. For me it is an up-beat exercise experience to music. Since my ministry to families requires that I travel extensively four to five months a year, I also schedule a luncheon date with a friend each week I am home. In the middle of the week, when I am inundated with writing deadlines, letters to answer, phone calls, and contracts to sign, I walk off, leaving it all behind. There will always be one more book to write. But if I don't make time for friends, if I don't make staying in touch with them a priority, they will quickly forget me. I have a birthday bunch that gets together regularly, quilting friends, and a group I go antiquing with.

If you have always longed to take oil painting lessons or do more entertaining, it all begins with scheduling time for yourself on your weekly calendar.

3. Vary leisure activities. Leisure activities should include new and fun things to do. Repeating the same activity over and over, even if you enjoy it, could become routine and boring. Studies suggest that those who invest time in pursuing new interests have a greater sense of well-being than those who keep doing the same things again and again.

For an activity to be truly relaxing it should be totally different from what is done during the workday. If you have a high-pressure, intensely competitive job, choose low-pressure, noncompetitive activities. Those who have desk jobs in which sitting is the chief activity should think of a more active leisure time. If you work by yourself most of the time, you would be stimulated by an activity that puts you near interesting people and a place buzzing with activity. And those who have the stimulation of a crowded office might want to engage in an activity that provides peace and solitude.

> *There is nothing better for a [woman] than to enjoy [her] work.*
> ECCLESIASTES 3:22

The author part of my life goes against my sanguine personality. I work at home, where my only human contact is with Harry and my secretary, who comes in two days a week. My outgoing nature cries out for happy people, continuous playful fun, and constant activity. Fortunately, my choleric nature forces me to stay at home and write, since my living depends to a large degree on writing. But some days I get so desperate for contact with the outside world that I literally pray for the phone to ring. This is not an interruption, but a means by which I can stay in touch with civilization. Therefore, my weekly Bible study group, Jazzercize class, and lunch with friends serve as vital links to my sanity. The travel and teaching part of my work serves my personality well.

4. Take time to be alone. Barb yearned for some time alone once in a while. Growing up, she shared a bedroom with a younger sister. Now she is married to an adoring physician husband and is the mother of three, and still longs for occasional time alone. One incident sums up her feelings. Brian was scheduled to take all three children shopping one night. Barb figured she had a good two hours to herself, so she settled down with a cup of tea and a good book. Ten minutes after they left, she heard the garage door open. Brian had forgotten the checkbook. Since he had to return home, he called off the entire shopping trip, sending Barb from total contentment to absolute resentment in 10 minutes.

Barb isn't the only one suffering from a lack of alone time. Many women face the same dilemma. They long for time to themselves; but the demands of career, family, friends, home, church, and community crowd out time alone.

Some women think of privacy as an expendable luxury. The first thing working women sacrifice is time for private pleasure. This is particularly true for lower-paid working mothers. Even when women do seek time out, they are usually still "on call." For some reason, women's time is more easily interrupted than men's time. For example, a man will sit down to watch TV, blocking out everything else. A woman will sit down to watch TV if the laundry is done, the kids are in bed, the dishes are in the dishwasher, the floor is swept, lunches are made, the bathroom is straightened, the phone isn't ringing, breakfast is laid out for the morning, and the family room is picked up. Even then she may think of what she might be doing while she is watching TV!

Private time may be more necessary to some women than others, but all women need some time to call their own. Research points to the fact that we can't ignore our need for privacy and stay healthy. When we don't take time to recharge our batteries, the result is privacy deprivation, a prime source of negative stress. Chronic stimulation and overwork lead to fatigue and deplete the immune system. Chronic high stress can eventually lead to physical illness.

A 12-year study of 1,200 men and women attending a night school program found that persons who endured high-stress jobs during the day, then studying and attending class at night and raising families, reported more illnesses when they didn't take time for relaxation and leisure time activities, than when they did. These students neglected other personal needs also, such as exercise and proper nutrition.

Privacy deprivation hurts your emotional well-being, causing an accumulation of resentment, moodiness, depression, and eventually total burnout. You'll find that when you neglect personal time, your children will annoy you, and you won't feel like being intimate with your spouse. Sex has little appeal to an overworked, stressed woman.

Need for private time varies, depending largely on one's personality and lifestyle. Introverts require more time alone than extroverts People who work alone may desire less privacy than those who work in public arenas throughout the day. Those suffering from deep grief may also need more time alone. Whatever your situation, work some private time into your schedule.

5. *Make the most of unexpected bits of time.* Moments for ourselves don't always have to be scheduled. Unexpected bits of time can be captured and pleasantly used to advantage, such as waiting for a doctor's appointment or sitting in a traffic jam. Carry a book, a cassette, quilting, or some handwork for just such an occasion. Rather than sweating the delay, grab the minutes that are unexpectedly yours and use them as you like.

6. *Use commuting time creatively.* Should you commute to work daily, or even drive children to school or music lessons, use such time to your advantage for something you and the children enjoy. Perhaps you long for the opportunity to curl up with a good book but lack the time. Buy the book on cassette and listen while driving. It just might become a pleasant method of quieting the kids and educating all of you.

If you commute alone, you might think of using this block of time for personal devotions. Listen to a devotional tape or one that teaches how to memorize scripture. Then put on soft background music and finish out your commute with prayer.

For the past two years my daughter, Carlene, has been driving her four boys 33 miles to school. Four boys might get a little rowdy on a 45-minute ride twice a day. But she has trained (note the word "trained") her children to listen to cassettes. Together they have listened to dramatized Bible stories (she now knows the stories as well as they do), *Lake Wobegon Days,* and the best of camp meeting speakers. They have also listened to my book *The Compleat Tween—A Guide to Growing Up for the 9- to 14-Year-Old.* This provided an excellent opportunity for sex education and discussion. She'd stop the cassette at times, ask questions, and discuss the topic at hand.

I belong to a service that provides me with interviews of professionals on cassette—a fast and easy way to obtain credits in my field of expertise.

7. *Take five—whenever you can (or several times a day).* Your schedule may be demanding and time pressures so great that you can't take an afternoon, or even an hour a day, to enjoy leisure-time activities. Large chunks of time may always be difficult to come by, but everyone can find five-minute time bites. When you work in an office, the law grants you a 15-minute break every two hours. Why? Research shows that accidents decline and productivity increases when regular breaks are taken from work.

So treat yourself to several five-minute leisure intervals throughout the day.

8. *Make ordinary tasks fun.* Ordinary tasks are always there, awaiting attention. Some of these tasks are mundane or downright unpleasant. Yet they must be done. Our attitude toward ordinary tasks can be improved by setting the task up to become more pleasant.

Here's how it works. Few of us enjoy cleaning bathrooms. So how can bathroom cleaning become more enjoyable, or even fun? By adding the right details. Inhale and savor the smell of "clean" as you use cleaners. Take pride in the shine of the mirror and countertop. As you complete the job, spray a little elegance with a scented spray.

In your bedroom, don't just make the bed and run. One third of your life is spent in this room. Care for your bedroom so that it becomes pleasurable. When I redecorated several years ago, I began with our bedroom. With its soft, soothing colors, I still consider it one of the most beautiful rooms in my home. While cleaning this room, I might add a bouquet of flowers, light a fragrant candle, or add an elegant lace pillow to the bed. Maybe I savor the watercolor pictures that hang over the bed—pictures of blossoms my mother painted while she was in high school.

Some other suggestions:

Now and then it is good to pause in our pursuit of happiness and just be happy.
ANONYMOUS

- Letter writing will be more enjoyable if you have beautiful stationery and write with colored pens.
- When reading a book, record on the flyleaf where you got it, from whom, and the date you read it. Add the name of the one who recommended it and savor your friendship.
- When cleaning, put on something pretty, daring, or even sexy.
- When cooking, put on a pretty apron.
- Put some fresh flowers on the table. Use a new set of dishes or new placemats.
- When vacuuming, blast your favorite Billy Ray Cyrus music loudly.
- Do a fancy two-step while dusting.
- Light a fragrant candle in the bathroom while cleaning the toilet.
- Sing a silly song while you reorganize a drawer.
- Make bill paying more pleasurable by ordering checks in a design that suits your personal taste.

These small touches, added to everyday chores, can make them almost fun, elevating mundane to special. When you take a second to readjust your attitude and add the right details, you may begin to enjoy daily tasks.

As you do so, you are making a personal statement about yourself. And giving yourself a marvelous sense of well-being. When the little things in our lives are satisfying, outside pressures and disappointment are easier to take.

Even doing this much makes you feel better about yourself. You'll be more useful to others and more at peace with yourself. By adding pleasant touches of beauty and fun to everyday activities, you'll make better use of your time, stimulating enthusiasm and providing you with more energy and a happier spirit.

9. *Take a humor break.* Medical science tells us that humor and laughing are good for what ails us. One specialist has dubbed laughter as "internal jogging." It's well known that laughing prevents heart attacks, promotes longevity, relieves stress and tension, and aids in the healing of cancer and other illnesses.

Norman Cousins, in his popular book *Anatomy of an Illness*, writes, "I 'laughed' my way out of a crippling disease that doctors believed to be irreversible." He undertook such a radical remedy after reasoning, "If negative emotions produce negative chemical changes in the body, wouldn't the positive emotions produce positive chemical changes?"

> *If you experience stress, you're doing it wrong.*
>
> JAY CONRAD LEVINSON

It worked. Cousins found that 10 minutes of genuine belly laughter served as an anesthesia and gave him at least two hours of pain-free sleep. He discovered significant scientific research on the physiological benefits of laughter that stimulates endorphins.

It has been estimated that one needs 12 laughs a day to stimulate the endorphins and remain healthy. Three of those laughs must be belly laughs—the kind that begin down deep and rumble on up, the kind of laugh that makes you tilt your head back and let 'er rip. If you aren't laughing 12 to 15 times a day you are underlaughed.

Dr. Joyce Brothers writes that humor "lets us detach ourselves from our troubles, laugh at them, and eventually overcome them." She says that "studies indicate that those who lack a sense of humor are short on emotional stability, self-confidence, and the ability to endure stress. Those with a good sense of humor tend to be more resilient and are able to cope better." Perhaps we had better take more seriously the text that reads, "A merry heart doeth good like a medicine" (Prov. 17:22).

Some tips for getting more laughs out of life:

- Share a funny story that you read or hear. Fabricate (or exaggerate, if necessary) to get the giggles going.
- Play with words. Rather than taking everything at face value, look for double meanings. Practice puns.
- Tell a joke. You don't have to be a comedian who can bring the house down. Master one-liners like this one: "Q: Why did the children of Israel wander in the wilderness for 40 years? A: Even back then men wouldn't stop and ask for directions!" Oh, well. A bad joke is better than no joke at all. The goal is to laugh. Even at something silly.
- Read books that contain elements of humor. I was never an Erma Bombeck fan until I read her book *When You Look Like Your Passport Photo, It's Time to Go Home*. For anyone who travels as much as I do, she is at her hilarious best. Or perhaps you might enjoy a loving but hilarious look at her 45-year marriage to a man who would finish her sentences (*A Marriage Made in Heaven, or Too Tired for an Affair*).

Laughter is a great tranquilizer for problems and stress. Stop being so serious—start laughing today. Someone has said, "If you are happy, notify your face!"

10. Value beauty. Beauty has healing power for stressed lives. Surround yourself with beauty, and watch what happens to your spirits. Appreciate an elegantly set table with fine china; a painting that brings joy; fresh flowers, artfully arranged; quality fabrics; trims of battenberg lace; a finely crafted table. Look for the rainbows in life. Once you develop an appreciation for the beautiful things, you can develop deeper sensitivity for beauty. Since I became aware of this principle, I have become more convinced God has built into each of us an appreciation for beauty and color. Our definitions of beauty may differ, but this is what makes life more interesting.

When stressed to the max and near the point of brokenness, surround yourself with beauty. Beauty, whether God-made or human-made, helps restore us. Celebrating beauty brings meaning out of the mundane.

It may be difficult to feel entitled to a little pleasure when caught in the press of multiple demands. But taking care of personal needs instead of continuously suppressing them to tend to the needs of those around you is the source of energy to cope with multiple demands. Endless complaining about your lot in life, focusing on your problems, and concentrating on your frantic pace saps energy. Put Secret to Sanity 7 into effect today by taking 10 minutes to make some portion of your life fun and enjoyable.

How about starting right now? A few hours can make a great difference! Turn the page to find out how to stop the world and smell the roses.

---

[1] Donna Christiano, "The Best Years of Our Lives," *Ladies' Home Journal,* November 1994, p. 62.

[2] Juliet B. Schor, *The Overworked American: The Unexpected Decline of Leisure* (New York: Basic Books, 1991), pp. 83-105.

[3] Diane Fassel, *Working Ourselves to Death: The High Cost of Workaholism, the Rewards of Recovery* (San Francisco: Harper's, 1990).

40 FABULOUS FUN WAYS
TO STOP THE WORLD AND SMELL THE ROSES

1. **Send your husband and the kids to Taco Bell for supper.** And to Baskin-Robbins afterward for an ice-cream dessert (your treat), while you curl up with a three-handkerchief book.
2. **Turn your bathroom into a luxury spa.** Hang up a "Do Not Disturb" sign and pamper yourself rotten with accessories, such as an inflatable bath pillow, scented bubble bath, oversized sponges, and a huge fluffy towel. Play your favorite soothing music.
3. **Plan a vacation.** Really need to get away for a vacation but can't do it now? Stop by a travel agency and take a peek at specials currently available. *Begin planning your next vacation immediately.* Just getting this far will lift your spirits.
4. **Listen to some great classics.** Driving home during heavy traffic can be tough, especially if dinner isn't planned. Instead of increasing your stress level by listening to a political talk show or a news report on crime, calm your nerves with some great classical music. Some suggestions:

Grieg	*Peer Gynt* suite
Debussy	*Prelude to the "Afternoon of a Faun"*
Brahms	Piano Concerto No. 2 and Violin Concerto in D Major

5. **Buy a bouquet of flowers.** Do you long for sunshine on a rainy day? Treat yourself to a colorful bouquet of flowers. Let their fragrance smile at you from your desk all day, then from your table at home during the evening.
6. **Go on a mini shopping spree.** They say the best things in life are free. But right next to that in popularity is a mini shopping spree. Head for the mall and check out that lingerie shop you've never dared investigate. Try on (or at least hold up) a piece or two of something slinky. This will bring a smile to your face!
7. **Bake something quick and easy that makes the house smell heavenly.** My personal pick for a fast and super-easy treat is Congo Bars. Preparation time is only a few minutes:

Congo Bars

Mix together and cool:	1 lb. brown sugar
	⅔ cup margarine
Mix together in bowl:	3 eggs (beaten)
Add:	Melted brown sugar and margarine
	2⅔ cups flour
	2½ tsp. baking powder
	1 cup walnuts, chopped
	2 cups chocolate chips

Pour batter into 9" x 13" pan sprayed with nonstick spray. Bake 25 to 30 minutes at 350°F. Cut into squares and enjoy—a real family treat.

8. **Take a long walk under a pretty umbrella during a spring rain.** Smile and nod to each primrose, crocus, daffodil, or tulip that greets your eyes. Thank God for the promise of another spring and all the seasons that follow.

9. **Too tired to clean house?** Too exhausted to complete even one household task? Been that way for a week or longer? Be good to yourself: Hire a housecleaning service to get your house in shape. Spend the next few days savoring the feeling a clean home provides.

10. **Do something completely different and unexpected, just to change your routine, scenery, and tempo.** Try a Jazzercize class or sign up for a floral arranging class. Go to a Western music concert or stroll through an art museum.

11. **Take a few minutes to sort through a stack of recipes you've been saving and meaning to try.** Surprise your family or friends with a new gourmet masterpiece.

12. **Have an urge to browse?** Head for a flea market or an estate sale in search of a prize collectible at a bargain price. What collectibles are most valued right now? Old toys, dolls, teddy bears, Depression-era glass, old kitchenwares, folk art, and quilts.

13. **Take a walk on the wild side.** Visit your local zoo. Make funny faces at the monkeys. Rename the animals after those persons who cause you the most stress. Indulge in a gooey caramel candied apple and return home feeling refreshed.

14. **Challenge your mate or a friend to a game of tennis and head for the courts.** It's a good way to slam your frustration out. (The loser buys lunch.)

15. **Take a hike!** When the pressure gets too much, pack picnic fixings and head for the nearest state park. Take a hike, literally. An afternoon away from it all will bring perspective to the pressures of life.

16. **Born to shop but short on cash?** Look for a sensational bargain in a discount store.

17. **Create something crafty with your hands.** Sharpen your knitting needles and start a new sweater. Design a silk floral arrangement for the dining room table. Begin a quilt from scraps in your fabric library. So what if it takes a year or more to complete? Pleasure comes from beginning a project you consider fun. It renews and refreshes one's spirits.

18. **Call a friend and chat for 10 minutes.**

19. **Spend $20 on something you wouldn't ordinarily spend money on.** You're worth it.

20. **Sit in an empty church and meditate.** Study the scenes depicted in the stained-glass windows. Meditate on a favorite passage of scripture that brings peace. Pray; leave your problems with the Eternal One. Sense the fullness of His power and strength.

21. **Hang a "Do Not Disturb" sign on your bedroom door (after you settle the kids down with their favorite video).** Lie down with your feet up for 10 minutes.

22. **Pamper your nails and your spirits.** Treat yourself to a manicure. You not only deserve it, you probably really need it.

23. **Go to the park and feed the ducks.** Toss them scraps of bread saved for the occasion. Watching them tip upside down to retrieve the morsels will make you smile and brighten your spirits.

24. **Pick (or purchase) a single perfect rose and put it in your most elegant bud vase.** Inhale the fragrance. Let the color, beauty, and scent remind you of your value in God's eyes.

25. **Do something for someone else.** Run an errand, purchase a gift, send

a card, or share some freshly baked cookies with someone who is down and out. You'll feel better realizing how well off you are!

26. **Stressed to the max but don't have time for a long, leisurely bath? A shower with a scent may be just the ticket.** According to a new study by the Smell and Taste Treatment and Research Foundation in Chicago, the scent of green apples reduces anxiety and the severity of migraines. The best way to inhale the aroma is in the shower, using one of the new green apple bath products. Try Alberto Culver *Fresh Apple* Shampoo, Bath & Body Works *Country Apple* Body Splash, or Naturistics *Green Apple* Glycerin Soap.

27. **Hint for a cold rainy night:** Put the kids to bed early and shuttle your husband off to the gym. Light a fire in the fireplace. Prepare a cup of chamomile herb tea, known for its healing effects. Play a favorite compact disk to soothe the stress from your soul. A new find is *Music for a Special Woman,** 45 minutes of enchanting classical music compiled expressly for women in need of feeling special.

28. **Rent a video to savor alone.** If you are tired of always getting your choice vetoed by the family and long for a video that would tickle your funny bone, try *Driving Miss Daisy.* Should you want a good cry, there's *Terms of Endearment.* For a total stress reducer you might watch *The Secret.*

29. **Rather than continuously playing the part of the servant to everyone in your household, pamper yourself.** Make an appointment for a facial, manicure, pedicure, or massage.

30. **Make your own wish list.** Reach for your personal planner and under "Personal" designate a page entitled "Wish List." Write down things you'd like to do that would bring you pleasure. Do you want to learn to quilt? learn a language? play the organ? rent a house at the beach for a week? go bird-watching? work in your flower beds? enjoy a leisurely lunch with a friend? take a cruise to the Caribbean? visit the Big Apple for two weeks? move to a country estate? hire a full-time housekeeper? have lunch at the Space Needle in Seattle? go to a spa for two weeks and lose 20 pounds? Keep writing until you have a list of 10.

31. **Try something new every day.** Wear a blouse that didn't come with the suit. Use a different place mat on the table. Switch objects from

two tables in your home. Change your hairstyle. Rearrange furniture. Use fruit for a centerpiece rather than flowers. Try a new recipe. Take a break from the routine. Free yourself to experiment rather than remaining locked into rigid patterns.

32. **Let your comic side cut loose.** Make a funny face or funny noises. Have a giggle fit. Laugh. Let your lighter side show.

33. **Find a peaceful refuge.** Every woman needs a place of refuge to call her own, a place that makes her feel safe from the pressures of life. For many women it's a special place in their home. Find or create that space, and enjoy.

34. **Play with your children.** Do something messy, such as finger painting. See what a few minutes' play will do for you!

35. **Date your mate.** Arrange for a baby-sitter without feeling guilty, and go out with your husband. Leave your worries behind. Smile and flirt with each other. Laugh. Share a soda and smooch a little. What can be better than this?

36. **While grocery shopping, stop at the floral section of the supermarket.** Let your senses dance over the splashes of color created by the chrysanthemums, azaleas, lilies, and hyacinths.

37. **Add a special touch to supper.** Buy a bunch of daisies for the table. Take one and lay it on each napkin. When your daughter asks, "What's this, Mommy?" tell her you are celebrating being *us.* Great role modeling! And a touch of loveliness makes a difference long afterward.

38. **Blast your favorite music on your stereo system.** Pretend that you are an award-winning ballerina as you twirl and two-step around the house.

39. **Take a 15-minute nap.** Set your alarm, then lie down for 15 minutes in your favorite room. Put your feet up. Let your mind take you to your favorite spot in nature or on a dream vacation.

40. **Invite a neighbor in for a cup of tea.** Relax, chat, and laugh. Enjoying a few minutes' reprieve from pressure will revive your spirits.

---

* *That Special Woman,* edited by Lois L. Kaufman and published by Peter Pauper Press in White Plains, New York, is paired with a collection of verse and a compact disk of enchanting classical music.

Time-out for Simple Pleasures

Assignments:

1. Schedule time on your personal planner for one pleasurable activity per week for the next four weeks. What would you like to do in an afternoon if you only had the time? Write those four things down.

Activity	Date	Time
1. _____	_____	_____
2. _____	_____	_____
3. _____	_____	_____
4. _____	_____	_____

2. For personal devotions read Ecclesiastes 8:15: "So I commend enjoyment, for there is nothing better for people under the sun than to eat, and drink, and enjoy themselves, for this will go with them in their toil through the days of life that God gives them under the sun" (NRSV).

This verse says to me: _____

_____

_____

As a result of what this verse tells me, I will _____

_____

_____

Laughter is the brush that
sweeps away the cobwebs of the heart.

AFFIRMATION
for Secret to Sanity 7

Today I choose to put order in my life.
I will make time for myself at
least one time per week. I will forget
schedules and work and do something
I enjoy just for fun. I will let something
go if necessary and make taking time
for myself a priority.
It can be done, and life can be fun!

Lift your spirits—go the extra mile

1. Send a greeting card that expresses love and appreciation to your spouse, a child, or a special friend. Plan for it to arrive as a surprise and make their day!

2. On your way to work, or when picking up the children from school, take a different route. This small change in a routine activity can make everything look different.

3. Get up a half hour early one day this week and go on a morning meditation walk. Praise God as Creator. Talk to Him about your day. Note God's beauty in creation as you walk. Look for an unexpected surprise. See if this one walk might become a daily habit.

4. Volunteer with enthusiasm to help with some project at church for which you can make a contribution. Watch the spirits of the existing group rise.

Today you have been given a fresh beginning.
This world is yours. Enjoy every moment of today.

THE CHALLENGE
FOR TODAY

A psychologist once surveyed some 3,000 people picked at random from a telephone directory. The survey was brief. It asked, "What have you got to live for?" More than 90 percent of the respondents stated they were *waiting*. Waiting for their marriage to improve, for their children to grow up, to become grandparents. They were waiting to retire and gain more leisure time. They were waiting for next year, or a dreamed-about tour of Europe. They were waiting for something exciting to happen. They were giving up today, waiting for the promise tomorrow held. These people failed to realize that today is the tomorrow they waited for yesterday!

It's a pity that we endure the present while waiting for some future event that may or may not ever happen. Each day is short, each hour flies by, each minute can be filled with life and something enjoyable. *Today* is here only once and will never return.

Are you enjoying *today? Today* you have been given a fresh beginning. *Today* you can open your eyes and find a new world. This world is yours. Enjoy every moment of *today,* it will soon be gone. Thank God for this new beginning!

Greet *today* with a smile. Make up your mind to be agreeable.

Breathe in the fresh, cool air and revel in the rays of sunshine. Beauty is God's therapy for the ugly side of life. Fear, anxiety, depression, and worry can be overcome with an appreciation of beauty.

Today is here. Don't think of what you would do if only things were different. Things are not different. They are what they are. This is the home you live in, and these are your circumstances. Make the best of what you have.

Instead of dreaming of what you'd do if you had the time, take time to make something happen. Dream, if you will, but work to make your dream come true. Do the things you should be doing, and stop doing the things you should not be doing.

Stop the flood of alibis. Stop saying "If I only had the time, I'd . . ." You'll never find time to do everything. Pick one thing you want to do, and do it.

Today is here, and it is yours. Act toward God and others as if *today* were your last day on earth. Life doesn't begin at 40; life begins when you take charge of your attitude and begin enjoying what you have.

It's never too late to become what you might have been.
GEORGE ELIOT

Only you can choose what you will do with your time and your life. Time can be your ally or your enemy. But your choices *today* determine your quality of life tomorrow. If you want freedom and happiness, you must fight for it *today*. It's only if you have your life and your home under control that you can truly make life happier for yourself and those around you.

Now is the time to make the hard choices necessary to accomplish this. The greatest gift you can give the people you love is you. Now is the time to develop high-quality relationships. Time must become your ally. Not only will you be a happier person; you will touch the lives of those around you in a positive way.

Your life as an organized woman begins *today*.

I'm cheering you on!

BIBLIOGRAPHY

Anson, Elva, and Kathie Liden. *The Complete Book of Home Management.* Chicago: Moody Press, 1979.

Aslett, Don. *Clutter's Last Stand.* Cincinnati: Writer's Digest Books, 1984.

———. *Do I Dust or Vacuum First?* Cincinnati: Writer's Digest Books, 1982.

———. *Is There Life After Housework?* Cincinnati: Writer's Digest Books, 1985.

———. *Who Says It's a Woman's Job to Clean?* Cincinnati: Writer's Digest Books, 1986.

Aslett, Don, and Laura Aslett Simons. *Make Your House Do the Housework.* Cincinnati: Writer's Digest Books, 1986.

Barnes, Emilie. *More Hours in My Day.* Eugene, Oreg.: Harvest House Publishers, 1982.

———. *Survival for Busy Women.* Eugene, Oreg.: Harvest House Publishers, 1986.

———. *The 15-Minute Organizer.* Eugene, Oreg.: Harvest House Publishers, 1991.

Conran, Shirley. *Superwoman.* New York: Crown Publishers, 1978.

Cox, Connie, and Cris Evatt. *Simply Organized! How to Simplify Your Complicated Life.* New York: Putnam Publishing Group, 1986.

Culp, Stephanie. *Conquering the Paper Pile-Up.* Cincinnati: Writer's Digest Books, 1990.

———. *How to Conquer Clutter.* Cincinnati: Writer's Digest Books, 1989.

———. *You Can Find More Time for Yourself Every Day.* Cincinnati: Betterway Books, 1994.

Dodd, Marguerite. *America's Homemaking Book.* New York: Charles Scribner's Sons, 1968.

Eisenberg, Ronni, and Kate Kelly. *Organize Your Home.* New York: Hyperion, 1994.

Engstrom, Ted W., and R. Alec Mackenzie. *Managing Your Time.* Grand Rapids: Zondervan Publishing House, 1967.

Evatt, Crislynne. *How to Organize Your Closet and Your Life.* New York: Ballantine Books, 1981.

Goldfein, Donna. *Everywoman's Guide to Time Management.* Millbrae, Calif.: Les Femmes Pub., 1977.

Guilfoyle, Ann. *Home Free: The No-Nonsense Guide to House Care.* New York: W. W. Norton & Co., 1984.

Hirsch, Gretchen. *Womanhours: A Twenty-one Day Time Management Plan That Works.* New York: St. Martin's Press, 1983.

Hoole, Daryl. *The Joys of Homemaking.* Salt Lake City: Deseret Book Company, 1976.

Klein, Ruth. *Where Did the Time Go?* Rocklin, Calif.: Prima Publishing, 1993.

Lew, Irvina Siegel. *You Can't Do It All.* New York: Atheneum, 1986.

McCullough, Bonnie. *Totally Organized.* New York: St. Martin's Press, 1983.

Peel, Kathy. *The Family Manager.* Dallas: Word, 1996.

Schor, Juliet B. *The Overworked American: The Unexpected Decline of Leisure.* New York: Basic Books, 1991.

Silcox, Diana, and Mary E. Moore. *Woman Time—Personal Time Management for Women Only.* New York: Wyden Books, 1980.

Skelsey, Alice. *The Working Mother's Guide to Her Home, Her Family and Herself.* New York: Random House, 1970.

Stoddard, Alexandra. *Creating a Beautiful Home.* New York: Avon Books, 1992.

———. *Daring to be Yourself.* New York: Avon Books, 1992.

———. *Living a Beautiful Life.* New York: Avon Books, 1986.

Uris, Auren. *Executive Housekeeping—The Business of Managing Your Home.* New York: William Morrow and Co., Inc., 1976.

Young, Pam, and Peggy Jones. *Sidetracked Home Executives.* New York: Warner Books, 1981.